Praise for *Spiritually Fierce*

"I believe that Ricci-Jane Adams is at the top of her profession, and her book commands our respect both for its fine-tuned guidance, and told in a most entertaining fashion. I have read *Spiritually Fierce* twice, and have recommended it to many as I believe that Ricci-Jane's book is arguably one of the finest in its field. I only wish I were in the area so I could attend one of Adams' seminars... With my whole heart I recommend that you buy it, read it, recommend it, and rejoice in the difference it will make in your life."

Jean Sasson, New York Times bestselling author

"Absolutely loved devouring this offering from new author Ricci-Jane Adams. Having known Ricci-Jane for a couple of years now I've been privileged to be on the receiving end of her teachings. I was delighted and excited to know this book was on its way and I wasn't disappointed when I started reading. A fabulous insight and practical guide into the art of intuition and equally just the right blend of science and spirituality."

Shannon Bush, Business Coach

"I read this book in one breath. I couldn't stop. I kept on screaming inside, YES! (Maybe out loud a couple of times too). I feel like I finally belong, like I've come home. Reading this book was a confirmation to me that I'm on the right path. Read this if you want to learn how to better connect to yourself."

Osnat Patton

"Ricci lovingly paves the way for you to meet your true self. She guides you with incredible support allowing you to step fully into your power, drop what does not serve you and absolutely fast-tracks your awakening. From my direct experience of following Ricci, becoming a student and reading her AMAZING LIFE CHANGING BOOK! It is like my soul has gone from travelling at horse n cart pace to the most glorious rocket ever! I am so deeply grateful to Ricci for inspiring me to show up more every day and regain my spiritual self-esteem in all it's glory!!! If you are craving so much more, know you're here to serve deeply and awaken through joy!"

Kristy Jamieson, Intuitive artist

"Spiritually fierce is an incredible book, beautifully written and full of deep wisdom. Ricci-Jane's words hold your hand as she leads you to a much deeper understanding of your own truth and power. She offers inspiration and concrete tools for your spiritual journey and she guides you through meeting and releasing your fears so that you can return to love. This book is a must read for everyone and I highly recommend it."

Jade Goodfellow

Spiritually Fierce

Are you ready to surrender to your unlimited self?

the
institute
for intuitive
intelligence

First published by Institute for Intuitive Intelligence in 2017.
This second edition published in 2018 by the Institute for Intuitive Intelligence

All quotes from *A Course in Miracles*© are from the 2nd Edition, published in 1997, by the Foundation for Inner Peace, P.O. Box 598, Mill Valley, CA 94942-0598, www.acim.org and info@acim.org.

Image of the EFT tapping points reproduced with copyright permission from thrivingnow.com

The 'how to' tapping guide information is reproduced with copyright permission from Nick Ortner. Taken from The Tapping Solution: http://www.thetappingsolution.com/what-is-eft-tapping

Spiritually Fierce

eBook format: 9780648095019
Print: 9780648095002
Cover design by Elise Elliot
Publishing services provided by Critical Mass
www.critmassconsulting.com

For Mama Angelique, who showed me my unlimited self from the very beginning.

Contents

The Spiritually Fierce Vow

I vow this day to meet my fear.

I vow to remember that I am unlimited, even when I feel separate and finite.

I commit to live with power and humility, strength and vulnerability, grace and grit, and to know that these qualities are the qualities of the Infinite, of which I am a divine piece.

I vow to live beyond the trinkets and superstitions of the new age.

I vow to remember that spiritually fierce is not just a phrase. Spiritually fierce is a movement of awakening consciousness of which I am vital part.

I give my life to the Infinite within me, above all else. I surrender all that is not of this truth.

I vow to live with the inner discipline, the soul fire that inspires me to choose love first. Every, single time.

A Note on Some Key Terms (and Especially the Use of the Word *God*)

Think about this section as a map. If we read the map before we begin the journey, we're going to have a much more easeful time getting where we are going.

Before we jump into meeting our unlimited selves, I want to clarify my use of the word *God*. As a researcher by trade, I am pedantic about language and how we use it. In the spiritual field, different people use a lot of the same words at different times; often it seems, without much reasoning behind their use. I want you to feel confident that I am using the terms I use with great care and consideration. Being an academic and a metaphysician, I am pretty much a spiritual geek and I am acutely aware of the *responsibility* of language. As an intuitive reader, this is essential to my work. I am turning spirit into matter through the bridge of language, and the care that I take has the power to transform the consciousness of my client. This is alchemy.

Back to the word *God*. In writing this book I spent a lot of time thinking about how to describe the unlimited consciousness of which we are all a part. I toyed with using terms such *Universal Consciousness, Divine Consciousness,* or even *Cosmic Consciousness.* These are all ways I have talked about God before, but they don't quite hit the mark. Plus, they are all a little wordy. I could also use *Source, Spirit,* or the *Universe.* What *God* means to me is <u>all</u> those terms (and I encourage you to find your own term that resonates for you), but using the word *God* is more effective and powerful to me in the context of this book.

I use the word *God* with great joy and deep love. I know that for many this word is complicated. My great hope is that you can forgo any fear or prejudice you have around this word and reclaim it for yourself, if that feels right. If not, put it aside with love. After all, as we will witness together, the *word* is innocent: it is our *belief* about it that gives it power.

In the meantime, I have another word I use throughout this book, which might make the idea of God more engaging. I use the word *Infinite* frequently. This is an attempt to describe what God – our unlimited selves – feels like. I use it as a verb and a noun. Infinite literally means limitless or endless in space, extent, or size; impossible to measure or calculate. This seems like an accurate description of God. Mostly we cannot describe God. We can only experience God and when we do we will come to know the substance of all that there is, the only thing that is real, and **that** is Love.

I use the term *the Universe* as well, and this is quite specifically meant to represent the physical reality we inhabit. The Universe is literally defined as all of time and space and its contents. It includes planets, moons, minor planets, stars, galaxies, the contents of intergalactic space, and all matter and energy. The size of the entire Universe is unknown, but the idea is the Universe began about 13.8 billion years ago, at the moment of the Big Bang. In my mind it stands to reason that understanding how the Universe – our home – works is vital, and we'll do just that in this book. It also applies that if there is a start date to the Universe, then there must be something that created the Universe. That's why I am more comfortable naming that *thing* as God, or the Infinite because it feels a bit bigger and bit older and, a bit more significant.

I also want to mention *consciousness*. It's a big concept and rarely well-defined. I want to make it clear how I am using it in this book. I use the term *consciousness* to describe the collection of beliefs we have, individually and collectively. Most of these beliefs are unconscious, inherited, tribal, and familial. The process of spiritual awakening is *raising consciousness*. We become aware of the contents of our consciousness as we awaken, and we raise it up out of the darkness and into the light, so we may investigate its contents and release what we don't need. Quite literally, we raise our beliefs from subconscious to conscious, to eventually return to the understanding that we are part of *one* consciousness.

That one consciousness is God. This is the end-point of recognising that we are unlimited. Perhaps at this point this raises more questions than it answers, but I invite you to come along with me, and bring an empty cup. The willingness to put aside what we think we know, to go beyond our current limits, is exactly where the miracles happen.

Oh, and I want to be <u>really clear</u> about the word *soul*. Our souls are defined as the immortal spiritual or immaterial part of us. This is so perfect, and I hardly need add any more, except to speak for a moment to the relationship between the soul and the human parts of us. It is my belief – and I am not alone in this – that the soul awakens to deeper and deeper awareness of its Infinite nature by coming into this human life and attending Earth School. Earth is a training ground for our souls and our souls can awaken through any conditions, but do not need to suffer in order to do so. That's up to us, and everything in this book is designed to show us how we can choose to awaken through love rather than fear.

Finally, let me clarify the term *ego*. I am really using the word ego from a spiritual perspective in this book. The Spiritual Science Research Foundation defines ego as:

> *Considering oneself to be distinct from others and God due to identification with the physical body and impressions in various centres of the subtle body. In short, ego is leading our life as per the thinking that our existence is limited to our five senses[1].*

Ego is the part of us that believes we are separate from God. It occupies a deficit mindset, and it truly believes it is keeping us safe by choosing from fear. Our job is make friends with the ego so it becomes part of our team for awakening. We simply need to get the ego back to its right size, so it can help us navigate Earth School. Without the right amount of ego, the world would be overwhelming to our soul nature. This book will show us how to get into right relationship with our egos and live our unlimited selves.

Introduction

The ego is afraid of the spirit's joy, because once you have experienced it you will withdraw all protection from the ego, and become totally without investment in fear.
— *A Course in Miracles*

Are you ready to meet your unlimited self? There is a good chance that as you are reading this book then the answer is yes, even if you don't know exactly what it means to be unlimited. I have an idea about what it is to be unlimited, and in these pages I am going to share the very steps I took – and keep taking – to unlimit myself.

This is a guidebook. It is highly practical. Every piece of knowledge is backed up by a replicable practice that I have used on my own path of becoming unlimited and wildly intuitive. The depth of the relationship we have with our intuition will be determined by the commitment we make to these practices.

Step one is accepting that we are intuitive because we are the same unlimited consciousness as God.

Step two is committing to living our life from this knowing. We are not chasing down our intuition, we are instead going on a spiritual adventure to understand what intuition actually is, how the Universe is truly configured, and discover we are already in possession of all that we need to live a life of unlimited consciousness.

Let's begin.

I have walked a very particular path to meet my unlimited self. My path is the path of intuition. I consider intuition to be the most powerful capacity we have to reconnect to our unlimited selves in every moment of our lives. Yet there are a number of roadblocks between our very natural, innate, intuitive power and us. These blocks, or problems, which as we'll see are not really problems at all, are the reason why we are largely disconnected from our unlimited selves individually and as a civilisation.

So, what are these blocks?

We have lost our spiritual self-esteem.

We hide from our spiritual nature, not because we don't believe it is real. We hide from it because we do not believe we are worthy of it. Caroline Myss, the great medical intuitive and contemporary mystic, states that without self-esteem we cannot become conversant in intuition. More than anything, intuition is the sign of a healed mind. The healing is of the belief in separation. If you know that you are one with all there is, how can you not have the answers to every question? To increase our intuition, we need to increase our self-worth. That is very confronting because we want to know what oracle cards to buy, or how to use the pendulum, or which crystal to work with. There is none of that here. We need nothing outside of ourselves. We are the oracle. We are entitled to have an unmediated relationship with God, and I will show us how.

There is only one impediment to us knowing that we are able to commune with the Infinite, and that is to overcome our fear that we are not worthy. This is what it is to be spiritually fierce. To be spiritually fierce is to surrender our limited selves, even though it will take courage and discipline, and sometimes mean we have to sit with discomfort. We have become afraid of experiencing discomfort. We avoid it at all costs. This is what spiritual discipline is, and the reward on the other side of the discomfort is great.

We are having the wrong conversation about intuition.

The way we think about it now is based on a schism, a duality that typifies how the Western consciousness has been evolving over millennia. Separation, rather than union. Duality – *this* or *that* – is the antithesis of union. It perpetuates the belief in our separation from one another and the Infinite. As such, we wrestle with truths that should be so ordinary as to be mundane. We question our soul's existence with the overly-privileged faculties of our minds, completely missing the point of our purpose on the planet. We are only allowed to be *this* or *that*. When I was little, we lived all over the world. I changed schools lots of times. I liked moving around, and I liked seeing new places. I never had any trouble making friends.

Something about it must have still affected me, though. There is something about not having one particular place to belong to. I used to have this recurring dream: I dreamt that I was in an airport or shopping centre, only ever partially-built, and across the mall or the departure lounge I could see my class of school friends being led by the teacher on some sort of excursion. The thing was, though, that I was with my *new* class going somewhere else. I would wave across the divide and try to have one group meet the other, but the faraway class never saw me, and the didn't hear me calling them. I would wake up in a panic. I wanted that divide to be filled; I wanted the two parts of my life to come together and see each other so that I wouldn't have to carry this enormous burden on my own: the burden of being divided in two.

There is a good chance that this dream says a great deal about the experience of being born into our human selves, and having to leave behind, or at least feeling as much, the "heaven" from which we depart. The experience of being human, especially as we begin to wake up to our soul-selves – and by that I mean when we recognise that the human drama of money, and work, and relationships, and worry is not all there is – can be traumatic, to say the least. We yearn for a union, without knowing how or with what. We long for a connection, a way to leap across the divide to unite the parts of ourselves.

We may feel, and I often did at that time, as though we have been abandoned to this earthly realm, and until we cross over at the end of our lives we are excluded from the experience of the divine in all its fullness. This is, however, the biggest illusion there is. All that ever was is now. All that ever will be is now. We are in the heaven that we seek, and we are already the spiritual masters we so desire to be. We have not left anywhere, and we are not going anywhere. We are already there. Duality simply is not real. We are this and that. Human and divine, and in this lies the secret to becoming unlimited.

As my dream describes, humanity adheres to a dualism that does not really exist, yet binds us to making impossible choices – secular or sacred, masculine or feminine, past or future, divine or human, virgin or whore, head or heart, light or dark. Life exists in the paradox of these seeming opposites. We have forgotten our true nature is union with all that is, and the only path to wholeness is to overcome dualistic belief. We are at war with ourselves, thinking away our creative energy, and disappearing deeper and deeper into the layers of illusion. We have become cleverer rather than more enlightened. Our cynicism grows as we access more and more knowledge. We are not awed and humbled by the magnificence of the Universe; instead, we seek to know it so we can control it.

None of our increasingly complex systems of belief – or dogma – have brought us any closer to being able to see through the darkness into the light that is the only constant and eternal truth. We are not spiritually fierce. We abandon our faith in a heartbeat for the comforts and superficialities of the new age. We always look outside of ourselves to find the cure, when all it really takes to be spiritually fierce, and live a life of truth, is to go within to the God inside of ourselves. Instead, we have built walls between God and ourselves and wonder why we have lost the deeper meaning of our lives. We have forgotten that we are one with the Infinite.

As a result, we are trapped in reductive conversations about our intuition. We seek the tools, the external trinkets, and the special magic belief systems that will give us intimate access to our intuition. Or, as is the way of Western civilisation, we dismiss it entirely. We dismiss it because we cannot resolve the spiritual paradox, and if we cannot command it with our minds, we cannot engage with it. We cannot find peace in the paradox. The greatest paradox of all is that despite all our denial of the divine, we are impossibly drawn towards it.

The crisis that brought me home

The biggest impediments to us knowing our unlimited selves are our lack of self-esteem and our belief in separation. I know this from deeply personal experience. This book is my story of reconciling the human and divine aspects of myself because no matter how I tried to forgo my Infinite self, the yearning of my soul would not let me go. Thank God for that. I had to figure out that the Infinite wanted less from me than it wanted to gift to me. I thought I had to suffer to inherit heaven on earth. For so many years on my spiritual path, I believed I had to overcome my human-ness. I located spiritual success as the transcendence of the human parts of myself, which I identified as being weak and broken. I struggled with this impossible task, of course. There is nothing that is not of God. To me, God is love. We all are. I was of the belief that I had to suffer to be worthy of that Infinite love - I had to overcome myself to meet God. It was nearly a decade ago now when the crisis happened. Collapsed over the vacuum cleaner on my living room floor, tears running down my face, I heard myself screaming to the blank ceiling:

Is this what I'm here for? Is this it?!

Burnt out, weary, joyless, lost, going through the motions, I found myself at a moment in my life that was empty. It wasn't empty of things to do. I was a single mother, completing a Ph.D., working part-time, even dating. Here I was in the depths of despair, screaming at an unknown higher power desperate for something to give my life meaning, all as I did the housework. I should have been happy - all the elements were in place. Instead, I was anxious, tired, stressed, and in despair. I was a hungry spiritual seeker devoted to learning more, working with teachers, reading all the books I could lay my hands on, but I was missing the point. I was building all my spiritual knowledge and practices on a faulty foundation. That's because I hadn't done the one thing that would truly bring me what I was looking for. I was adding spiritual trinkets and superstitions to my list of qualifications. I had not located God inside of myself. My self-doubt was my driving force because I had not taken the time to overcome my doubt, and to recognise that what I was seeking was *me*. Instead, I was always looking outside of myself for the answers.

Where there is doubt, intuition cannot reside. Does this mean we walk around in a cloud of our self-importance? Quite the opposite. An attitude of humility must also be cultivated to successfully access intuition in daily life because ultimately our awakening is an act of service.

How do we manage this strange paradox? It is, in brief, simply a matter of understanding where intuition is coming from and whom it will benefit. This happened for me in an instant. For years, even when working as an intuitive reader, I would feel anxious before going into a reading. *Would I be good enough? Would I be helpful? What if nothing happens?* My self-doubt made it all about me. Inevitably, each reading was exactly as it needed to be, and brought great comfort to the client.

My fear of unworthiness robbed me of the joy of being in service to my client. I knew my connection was clear and strong, but that wasn't enough. Then one weekend in 2015 I attended a workshop with one of Australia's best medical intuitives, Belinda Davidson. I was there with my mother and a group of around 60 women as we were introduced to Belinda's technique of reading the human energy field. The feeling in the room was clear and light. Belinda works with white light and was regularly channelling this light on our behalf. I was excited about what I was learning and how much of it was in line with my own process of reading. Investing in this professional development was part of my own personal commitment to keep on getting better at my craft, but what happened for me exceeded all my expectations.

At lunchtime on the second day, I was outside on the street in the winter sunshine standing by myself. Without warning, and in an instant, all my doubt was gone. I was filled from head to toe with certainty that *who I am* is unlimited consciousness. My spiritual self-esteem was suddenly intact. From that time on, I could feel the rightness of the information I shared with my clients, and in the work we did together, not because I was somehow improved, but because I was profoundly aligned with this truth:

I can of mine own self do nothing.

These words from the Gospel of John bring me home in an instant to my spiritual power. That moment on the street had in fact been years in the making. My constant prayer had been to remember my truth, to surrender to my unlimited self, and to experience what it was to be in a continual state of grace. My spiritual fierceness, which in this case was my unwillingness to give up even when I felt like I was running on blind faith, was suddenly met by the high vibration of that workshop and, in the spiritual leadership of Belinda. The paradox was reconciled, or more accurately, I found the peace within the paradox. I am everything and nothing. I did not have to fear that my connection in my readings was good enough because it was not even *me* doing the work. And yet, it was me. I am that I am. The relief was delicious. It was also the beginning of the end for me: the end of me working as a reader who answered people's questions about their lives, and as a healer who believed she could heal other people. I could not in good faith do what I knew was perpetuating other people's misery as it had mine. This was also the beginning of the creation of a method that I would one day teach others, that allows us to activate our own intuitive power and live it fiercely. It is a method that matches humanity where it is and it is what I will teach you now.

How to meet the times in which we live

We live in extraordinary times. The extremes of our age are both a reflection of our collective consciousness as a civilisation, and the medicine for us. In other words, this age is exactly that which humanity needs to take our collective, shared awakening higher. One measurable way that this is evident is in the recent sudden increase in Schumann Resonance, which according to Dr Joe Dispenza, research scientist at the intersection of quantum physics and neuro-sciences, act as a background frequency influencing the biological circuitry of the mammalian brain. Dispenza describes Schumann waves in this way: "As far back as we know, the Earth's electromagnetic field has been protecting all living things with this natural frequency pulsation of 7.83 Hz. You can think of this as the earth's heartbeat."[2] What is fascinating about the Schumann waves at this very moment in time is that they have increased so suddenly and so quickly. In January 2017, they shifted to 36–50 Hz. On April 16, 2017 this again increased to 90 Hz. On May 8, the frequency accelerated into the 120 Hz range. Dispenza hypothesises: "Since we are organic creatures made of matter and susceptible to electromagnetic fields, and because our lives are inseparable from the earth, then if the earth's frequency is rising, shouldn't that also raise our frequency?" The Schumann waves suggest that this exactly what is happening.

My belief is that the time of ambivalence is over. No longer can we sit in inaction and spiritual apathy. We are being invited to meet the times in which we live with the willingness to change and awaken. This gift of this time is accelerated change. We are being supported to awaken at a far more rapid pace than ever before. All the conditions support this if we are open to receive the blessing. How can we do this? What is being asked of us, and reflected in everything we see in our civilisation?

One of the greatest challenges we face is to become self-reliant. We look outside of ourselves rather than going within for the wisdom we seek. We have been taught that spiritual authority is external from us, and yet the formerly unquestionable power systems of our age – religious, political, and economic – are now unstable and inconsistent. We must now retrain ourselves not to seek outside for a magic bullet that will bring us into our spiritual power. The power is within; we are the Infinite. There is nothing else we need. Intuition is the gateway to that power. The good news is that we can easily find our way home when we navigate using our intuition. We simply need to change the conversation about intuition. We should begin here, with this question:

Do I know that I am pure, unlimited consciousness?

It is highly likely that the answer to that question for most of us is *no*. Let's work back from there, and establish how we became so very distanced from our innate, intuitive power.

Beyond *knowing* our intuition to *living* it

The purpose of this book is to connect us to our unlimited consciousness by demystifying intuition. Intuition is the language of God. It is our own, true guiding voice. To make intuition real again, as it was to the ancients, and as a compass to navigate the extraordinary age of our times, an act of reconciliation with our unlimited selves is required. It is not enough to know that we are intuitive. We must know how to trust that intuition and have the courage to take the action we are being guided to take. I call this *intuitive intelligence*, and it is a path for us to walk to return to our unlimited state if we choose to take it. It is an approach to living that is available to everyone. This is the path of the warriors of light, the soul-seekers, the spiritual change agents, the contemporary mystics, and the modern-day priestesses. Intuitive intelligence is a metaphysical approach and a liveable practice. It is spirituality *in the world*. It is what it is to live with spiritual fierceness.

The central tenet of this book is simple and powerful. We are all intuitive and we all have blocks to this intelligence that need to be cleared out so that we can have what we were born to have – a joyful unfolding of our soul's awakening. Life was never meant to be a struggle, but our disconnection from the God voice that is our intuition has caused us all enormous personal and global suffering. We do not trust ourselves, and we do not trust God. But with spiritual fierceness, practice, and devotion, we can find our way home to our bliss. Within these pages is an account of my personal path to living in that state of grace that typifies an awakened intuitive intelligence. The tools come from many ancient traditions, philosophies, and great contemporary teachers. The practices may not be new to you.

They are offered in a system that has been born of my own path and combined in ways that are designed specifically to activate intuitive intelligence. I have created this system because of the realisation that whilst most of us will agree that we are intuitive, this does not mean we live from our intuitive intelligence. We drop in and out of it. We require a system to lean into until it becomes habit. We are going against thousands of years of cultural and religious indoctrination that is within our cellular and collective consciousness. We are breaking habits of lifetimes to reclaim our personal power and a direct, unmediated relationship with God.

Intuitive intelligence is the practice of living our intuition. It has scientific evidence at its core. It is a heart-centred relationship with the world, and it takes as a given the quantum nature of reality. Gregg Braden tells us that we are in the "century of the heart".[3] The science of the heart's intuitive intelligence is evidence-based and peer reviewed. We will learn in this remarkable age to live from the heart's intelligence as a necessity for our collective survival, and shared evolution.

The Immutable Laws

The practices of intuitive intelligence are assembled around the three immutable Hermetic laws. The laws are drawn from *The Kybalion: Hermetic Philosophy*, originally published in 1908 under the pseudonym of the Three Initiates. This text contains the essence of the teachings of Hermes Trismegistus, also known as Thoth in Hellenistic Egypt. Thoth and Hermes were gods of writing and of magic in their respective cultures. Their laws open us to the deeper spiritual meaning of our lives. Just as the number three has sacred resonance for many spiritual seekers, the three immutable Hermetic laws are held in deep reverence by many of those on the path of awakening consciousness. Whether we consider them as allegory or fact, it matters not (even though quantum physics is now proving the efficacy of the laws), for adhering to the laws as metaphysics or quantum physics still yields the same powerful results. The governing system of Hermetic laws manages the cosmos and holds all things together. All things are ordered to the second. The Infinite is impartial. If our lives are not in accordance with how we want them to be, we simply need to ask, *how have I broken the law?* Intuitive intelligence is partnering with God, so we must know how the Infinite operates to activate our intuitive intelligence. This is what the laws are.

The three key sections of this book contain three turning points in my life. Onto each of these I apply an immutable law, and in so doing map my awakening to the intuitive intelligence within me. As I reviewed these turning points, it did not surprise me that they also correlated with the major archetypes of the divine feminine – maiden, mother, and wild woman/crone. Archetypal patterns align with intuitive intelligence powerfully, for intuition is symbolic. The patterns of meaning-making offered by understanding archetypes open us further to the sense of union between all. It takes us out of the personal and into a sense of shared experience that allows us compassionate resonance with the experience of others, without having to have lived their exact experience.

It is no surprise that this sacred number three keeps appearing. As we go on, we will also discover that there are three kinds of intuition, as defined by the leading- edge research organisation HeartMath Institute, and the contemporary mystic Caroline Myss. Each describes intuition as a multi-layered, dynamic experience that must be lived to be understood. It is the practices of intuitive intelligence that turned the Hermetic laws from knowledge to wisdom for me, and in so doing brought this wisdom into the full light of day so that I could indeed be the mystic without walls. In other words, the Hermetic laws made my spiritual practices real and applied. The question I asked of each law was the same – if this is the law by which the Universe abides, how may I make it work in my own life? A spiritual faith that does not bring my life into a continual state of grace is not a faith I want. And yet for some time this was the faith that I had. I used my spiritual seeking as a weapon against myself, instead of as a way to become unlimited.

I wanted a practical and robust faith that could not just withstand the reality of, well, *reality*, but also fill it with grace. I sought to make the laws as real as they could be for me by embodying them. Beyond the mind was where I sought to go, the mind that had held me a prisoner on my path of spiritual seeking, using my ever-growing knowledge to show me how I was getting it wrong. The Hermetic laws unleashed me from that prison of my own making and set me back on my path of devotion with a wealth of magnificent evidence that declared its truth. It was spirit meeting flesh, and all my previous spiritual darkness began to make sense. It's where my intuitive intelligence began.

Intuitive intelligence is light years beyond the question of "am I intuitive?". Instead, intuitive intelligence is the answer to these questions: *how do I live my unlimited self? How do I remember that I am God? What is required to live in partnership with my intuition in every moment?* This book answers these questions, and provides real steps on the path to meeting the pure unlimited consciousness within us all, so that we may inhabit our own intuitive intelligence with spiritual fierceness. Intuitive intelligence is a practice, the tools for which are provided here. It is a spiritual practice. Before going any further, ask yourself, *am I really ready to surrender to my unlimited self?* If the answer is no, I recommend you put this book down now. You will come back. It is inevitable. Intuitive intelligence is the answer to the call of our soul. We will, one day, if not today, all answer the call. It is the most powerful call we have ever heard, and every fibre of our being is yearning to respond.

Chapter 1

Intuitive Intelligence

Intuitive Intelligence is *living* our intuition. It is learning how to receive our intuition and then trusting ourselves and the Infinite enough to act on it. Intuition is nothing without intuitive intelligence. What is the point of possessing a superpower if you never have the courage to use it? Everything in our lives is improved when we are open to our intuitive intelligence. We get that long-desired upgrade to the first-class version of our reality. How does this happen? Ultimately, as is repeated throughout this book, intuitive intelligence is a sign of a healed mind. The healing is of the false belief that we are separate from – and less than – the Infinite by which we are created, or in other words, God. We are talking to God, and we finally realise that God is and always has been talking back to us, holding us, guiding us, and supporting us. We realise that we are a divine piece of a benevolent consciousness that is bowing down to our every command. When we live from our intuitive intelligence we are thinking like the Infinite: we are unlimited magnificence. We are one. The upshot of intuitive intelligence is that we no longer believe we are separate, finite, vulnerable, and isolated. We experience oneness as a natural and true state so that we are living our best life.

A warning here: when we switch on our intuitive intelligence everything is going to change. We are going to connect with a purpose and desire for our life that powerfully transcends what we think we want right now. It is unavoidable. When we open to our own transcendent nature as we partner with God actively, we are thinking like the Infinite. We are no longer held to the limits of three- dimensional human consciousness. We stop wanting only that which we can see at the limits of our current reality. This book comes out of the many intuitive intelligence workshops I have taught as part of my Institute, and the experiences of hundreds of people who have attended these workshops. Why is it that people choose to come and learn to activate their intuitive intelligence with me? What are they drawn to? There is a common theme to everyone who has come through the Institute for Intuitive Intelligence, the place I created from my own desire, and the school I would have wanted to attend at the beginning of my own spiritual awakening: they know that there is more. They have experienced something in themselves that has permitted them to see behind the veil of illusion. They have witnessed their own magnificence, their God-self, even if for a moment. When we witness this aspect of our own true nature it is impossible to unsee it. From that moment we know that life is more than we have been living. We know that we are capable of experiencing more than we are currently experiencing. We are ready to move beyond dogma and doctrine. Beyond gurus, beyond religion, beyond superstition, beyond trinkets, beyond wellness, beyond even self-awareness, which is not the same as meeting the divine within us – not at all. We know, even if only in fleeting moments, that we are that which we seek, we are unlimited, and we want to get to know our own incredible power.

When there is the option to remain in the illusion, however, or to set ourselves free with our new-found knowledge of our truth, remarkably, many, many people will choose to look away from their own brilliance. They don't want to take on the responsibility of being free. But you, and the many incredible students I have had the privilege of teaching, are one of the minority. You know you are more than this ordinary human reality would have you believe, and you want to look behind the veil. An activated intuitive intelligence will take you there. An activated intuitive intelligence throws the door wide open to the richness and fullness of our lives. It guides us towards the success we crave. It connects us to the peace we long for. It lovingly leads us to our life purpose and enjoins us to the people and places we need to bring our best life into fruition. Intuitive intelligence is s spiritual philosophy and a practice. It is a way to manifest our most joyful life, and a way to identify that life.

The formula for intuitive intelligence is:

Innate intuition + spiritual fierceness = intuitive intelligence

Spiritual fierceness is the quality that is required to bring intuitive intelligence to life. There is one word that is repeated again and again throughout the book – the word *practice*. It is impossible to surrender the old, subconscious, fear patterns that control us without a deep devotion and consistent practice. Eventually, practice with and to our devotional tools becomes effortless joy. We cannot imagine a life without these things, for not only do they enrich us for the time in which we engage with them, they bring us everything we desire all the time. It is how we make intuitive intelligence work. We must sweat the muscle of intuition to generate the spiritual heat that burns away the fear. Vishen Lakhiani of MindValley calls this *blissipline,*[4] because the reward for the effort is great. It is the peace that passes all understanding. I call it *spiritual fierceness*. It takes spiritual steel to beat ancient, culturally- indoctrinated addiction to fear. Spiritual fierceness is what allows us to be loyal to our own innate knowing, to defer to our own wisdom even when others doubt us. It is what is required to stare fear in the face and question it. It is the voice inside of us that asks: *What else is possible?* It is the courage to see the light when all others only see darkness. It is the state of flow we experience when we move beyond the belief in separation into a state of union with what we are.

In these coming pages we will journey together to learn how to overcome the blocks to our intuitive intelligence, and we all have these blocks. No matter where we are on the path with our intuition, we can go deeper. For to go deeper with our intuitive intelligence is to become more intimate with the Infinite. We are naturally intuitive and – in our fearless state –we are naturally trusting of the divine intelligence of God. Over time, we have learnt to distrust, but that is not our natural state. To attune to our intuitive intelligence, we don't need to acquire anything new. We simply need to remove whatever blocks our connection to *knowing, trusting* and *living* our intuition. To do this, we must know how intuition works, so let's find out now about the science of intuition.

Chapter 2

The Science of Intuition

There is a science of intuition, the way it works, the kinds and types of intuition, and the optimal conditions under which it flourishes. This chapter maps some of the best research and writing on the science of intuition. The information is designed to take us beyond the limits of the known, beyond the myths and superstitions to the cutting edge of the intersections of quantum physics and metaphysics. We do not live in a time that privileges the non-dominant sense of intuition, but that time is coming. The more we understand, the more power we must move beyond our limited selves. Importantly, I am keen to dispel the unhelpful myths about intuition that keep it maligned in our contemporary world and quarantined to the arena of the new age. It is, in fact, a *bona fide* superpower when understood and practiced. When the intelligence of our intuition is switched on, all our other intelligences increase including emotional, creative, and analytical. In every aspect of our lives, it serves us to understand and expand into our intuition.

One of the ways we can reclaim intuition as a valid – and in fact the most important – human intelligence is to know the science of how intuition works.

The three types of intuition

The HeartMath Institute is a research organisation that empowers individuals, families, groups, and organisations to enhance their life experiences using tools that enable them to better recognise and access their intuitive insight and heart intelligence. The institute tells us that there are three primary intuitions: implicit knowledge, energetic sensitivity, and nonlocal intuition.[5]

Implicit knowledge can be thought of as knowledge that has become second nature to us, as a result of continual experience or practice in a particular experience. For example, the car mechanic who can turn over a car engine and know, without further inspection, what is wrong with the vehicle. We can argue he has an intuitive knowledge of cars, which is correct, but it is knowledge that has been earned over time. His understanding of the car engine and the noises it makes and what they mean is implicit within him. His hunches are correct not because he is accessing information from the Infinite, but because he has spent a lifetime becoming intimate with the mechanics of car engines.

Energetic sensitivity refers to the "ability of our body and nervous system to detect electromagnetic and other types of energetic signals in the environment"[6]. Indeed, HeartMath have established that the human heartbeat of one individual can be detected via the body of another. People who identify as empathic or highly sensitive (also known as *empaths*) fall into this category. However, the truth is that we are all empathic and highly sensitive, and when we understand our electromagnetic biology, it becomes clear why. We are constantly collecting energetic information from one another, most often without realising it. When we are living the intuitive intelligence path there are powerful ways that this energetic sensitivity can be part of our toolkit for living in extraordinary times. Rather than being something that makes us too sensitive to inhabit the world, we begin to understand the information that is provided to us through this kind of intuition, and how to use it to our advantage.

Implicit knowledge and energetic sensitivity are part of our innate, local unconscious, pattern recognition, and biological intuition. These intuition types sit alongside the third kind of intuition, what HeartMath calls *nonlocal intuition*. I am most interested in talking about this kind of intuition, for this is the intuition I associate with intuitive intelligence. It is knowledge that is come by without reason or deduction. It is not confined by time and space, because by its very nature it is unlimited.

Nonlocal Intuition

Nonlocal intuition is defined by HeartMath as the type of intuition:

> *which refers to the knowledge or sense of something that cannot be explained by past or forgotten knowledge, or by sensing environmental signals. It has been suggested that the capacity to receive and process information about nonlocal events appears to be a property of all physical and biological organization, and this likely is because of an inherent interconnectedness of everything in the universe.*[7]

I think of it as the intimate conversation with the Infinite of which we are a part. As a rigorous scientific institute, HeartMath are far more cautious. They state that as yet there is no theory of nonlocal intuition, but the research is growing, and quantum physics goes a long way to help us understand the concept of nonlocal. In addition, as the Hermetic laws demonstrate, the idea of the nonlocal is ancient. Researcher Ervin Laszlo states:

> *The latest theories in quantum physics suggest that the space-time realm is not all there is: there is a deeper dimension in the cosmos. Consciousness could reside in that dimension, and only manifest itself in space and time. This insight has been known for millennia. Philosophers of the mystical branch in Greek metaphysics differed on many points but were united in affirming the existence of a deep or hidden dimension. For Pythagoras this was the Kosmos, a trans-physical, unbroken wholeness, the prior ground on which matter and mind, and all being in the world arises. For Plato it was the realm of Ideas and Forms, and for Plotinus "the One".[8]*

Deepak Chopra states that we are nonlocal entities having a local experience. What exactly does this mean? It is useful to explore this briefly so that we may better understand what is meant by nonlocal intuition. Nonlocal is defined as direct interaction of physical objects that are not in proximity. Quantum physics states that isolated particles can communicate nonlocally at the quantum level. Beyond the level of the sub-atomic particle, this still holds true. In other words, we can experience this in our inter-personal relationships.

Our local, limited perception leads us to believe in space and time as hard facts, yet all is occurring in oneness, or as Chopra says, "one gigantic nonlocal activity". Deepak goes on to state that:

Even though you think you see yourself in a mirror, you are actually seeing one state of your physical body. That one state, accessible through the five senses, isn't the whole. The whole also includes the quantum state of the particles that make up your body. The same holds true for the entire cosmos and reality itself.[9]

Most studies of intuition have to date only measured the local forms of intuition, including implicit knowledge and energetic sensitivity. The leading-edge science led by HeartMath Institute, Gregg Braden, Joe Dispenza, and Bruce Lipton, amongst others, is taking us to a new frontier in understanding what metaphysics has always known to be true and contributing to an evidence base for nonlocal intuition. We are Infinite unlimited consciousness masquerading as physical form.

For example, in proposing an emerging theory, Raymond Bradley of HeartMath Institute powerfully articulates the action of nonlocal intuition, His theory describes what is happening when we connect to nonlocal intuition. This theory is born of experiments designed to understand the success of repeat entrepreneurs. The study, conducted in partnership with Australian Graduate School of Entrepreneurship, explains:

How the entrepreneur's passionately-focused attention directed to an object of interest (e.g., a future business opportunity) attunes the bio-emotional energy generated by the body's psychophysiological systems to a domain of quantum-holographical information, which contains implicit, energetically-encoded information.[10]

In layman's terms, what this means is that when we focus our feeling state, we tune into a domain beyond the world of the senses, described here as "quantum-holographic information", that contains information that is energetically encoded. In other words, it is our consciousness meeting a far more unlimited consciousness and knowing what could not be known locally. What is very clear is that no matter what the subject we focus on, the act of tuning into non-local intuition is an active partnership. It is attuning to the Infinite.

We hold the vibration that allows us to tune into the vibration of the Infinite, or to use Bradley's language, the quantum- holographic. From my perspective, the information received via nonlocal intuition is God-mind consciousness, and whilst it is innate within each of us, it requires a level of discipline to activate it in a masterful way. It is us in communion with the Infinite, and we must want this communion.

Survival, Creative, and Visionary Intuition

Caroline Myss discusses intuition as three separate types that include survival intuition, creative intuition, and visionary intuition.[11] Both HeartMath and Myss' systems are useful ways to become intimate with intuition at work in our lives.

Survival intuition is with us from birth and resides in our solar plexus. This is what we call gut instinct, because we literally experience this intuition bodily and energetically in our solar plexus. This is because it relates to our sense of power and safety. Survival intuition alerts us to danger in a place, it is the mother's instinct that something is wrong with her child, or our instant awareness of whether we like or dislike someone. This level of intuition exists because life protects life. It is not spiritual, but until we pay attention to this intuition and act on it, the next levels of intuition cannot develop.

It takes a great deal of energy, and of will, to ignore our gut instinct, and yet some people live their whole lives in this way. This is because even at this level, our intuition – and ability to act on our intuitive hits – is connected to our self-esteem. Interestingly, this is also a quality connected with our solar plexus chakra. If we do not trust ourselves, we cannot trust our intuitive knowing, because it is emerging from us. On a side note, addiction of every kind is oftentimes the attempt to conceal our survival intuition from ourselves.

I make it a practice when I am driving that if I get an intuitive hit to turn right when I would normally go left at that intersection that I do not doubt it. I do not ask why. And I do not worry if I never discover the reason. My job is to trust my survival intuition, because I trust myself, because I trust the Infinite, and it has never steered me wrong. If, however, I had doubt in my own worth it is clear how easy it would be to ignore that intuition and end up in situations that did not serve me or are downright dangerous. I remember one night as a young woman I was out with a friend at a bar. It was late. We were out of money but keen to continue our festivities, so I offered to walk down to the ATM to get some cash.

As I stood at the ATM with my back to the street I felt someone stand behind me in the queue. A normal enough thing to happen at an ATM, but I also knew instantly that I was in grave danger. I didn't stop to look around, ponder if I was being paranoid or hesitate. I hit cancel on the machine, grabbed my card, and ran without looking back until I was safely back in the bar. Can I know if I was truly in danger, or if it was an overactive fear response to being out on my own late at night? To me it is very clear. Because I make a habit of honouring my intuition and seeing how well it serves me, I could also trust myself enough to act in that moment.

How many times have we heard people say, "I knew something was wrong, but I didn't listen to myself", or "that person didn't feel okay, but I went with him anyway", and so on. I have heard it a thousand times. When we do not trust ourselves we do not take action on our own behalf. We don't want to appear difficult, or impolite or contrary, so we deny our intuition to make sure we are liked and don't cause a fuss. This level of intuition should be so normal that it is mundane. Yet, even at this level we have trouble permitting the idea that there are non-dominant sense ways of receiving the deeper meaning of the world. So wedded are we to our dominant five senses that we do not trust our inner knowing.

The next level of intuition is creative intuition. At this level, our self-esteem plays an equally important role in our capacity to hear and trust our intuition, but at this stage we are actively co-creating rather than simply responding to the world. Myss says that with creative intuition we must become mindful of and consciously develop our tools for co-creation, because co-creation is a conscious effort. Whilst survival intuition is rudimentary, creative intuition is by design. We have come to an awareness that we are active participants in the creation of our life and awakening to the knowing that life will makes choices for us if we don't. This level of intuition is the place in which we must make a choice for our nonlocal consciousness first, and physical second. In other words, we are awakening to the inner world of symbolic intuitive sight and accessing the deeper meaning of the events of our life. We are awakening to where we truly create our lives.

To fully realise our creative intuition, or our co-creative intuition – the dialogue between the Infinite and us – we need to deepen our self-esteem once more. To evolve beyond the rudimentary survival intuition, we need to move out of simply reacting to the world and taking everything personally. This is the beginning of us creating our lives in partnership with the Infinite, or God. This is where we feel creative energy – or inspiration – enter us, and we take action with that creative energy. If we are still in our self-doubt, then we may pretend we did not hear that intuitive inspiration, or we will argue with ourselves that it is not possible. When I was twenty-four years old, I moved to a city I had never been to before, without a job or a place to live. I was so certain of my intuitive knowing, the inspiration that was co-creating this action with me, that I never wondered if it was the right thing to do or not. I knew. That move changed the course of my life. It was literally a leap into the unknown. I didn't know what I was meant to do in that place. I had left behind my entire life, including my job, but I didn't need to know what lay ahead. Every step was guided. As I sat outside my new favourite Italian espresso bar one morning shortly after my arrival, sipping my latte, I opened the newspaper to a page with an advertisement for a graduate course at the University of Melbourne. In that instant I knew I wanted to go back to study. Even though I wasn't eligible for the course I saw advertised, I applied anyway. For no reason I could ascertain, the head of the school took me under her wing and guided me towards the right qualification for me. She continued to be my biggest advocate and supervisor for many years as I went onto to complete my doctorate.

The final level of intuition discussed by Myss is what she calls visionary intuition. The best way to illustrate this kind of intuition is to continue the story from my own life. The powerful part of this creative intuition story above came much later, when I realised something much bigger was at work than just my limited self. I thought I was doing my Ph.D. because I wanted to be a university lecturer. I was totally on that track. But several years after my doctorate was complete I was stalling. I couldn't find the kind of work I wanted to do and the life I thought I was qualified for was disappearing before my eyes. Even though I had done my doctorate on the subject of magical realism, as a sneaky way to talk about spirituality in that ivory tower institution, I was fully expecting that my life as an academic would come to pass, because everything up to then had fallen into place. But I was wrong. The Infinite was preparing me for something much bigger than a job. I was being prepared for my life purpose. It didn't take too long for me to end up as the head of my own teaching institute, and the high-level qualification I received has prepared me to lead the revolution in excellence in my non-regulated industry. I did not know what I was training for. But I am continually grateful for the visionary intuition that took me there.

At any point I could have judged the individual events as not good enough, or as though something had gone wrong. Instead, at each step I could sense that there was a bigger pattern or a deeper meaning. I would often say that I could feel this bigger picture of my life even though I could not see the details. I kept moving in the direction I was being called. Visionary intuition is, according to Caroline Myss, acquiring the final initiation. It is when we know that we are simply the caretakers of a vision that wants to emerge through us. Are we willing to surrender our personal will to the vision of the Infinite, without necessarily knowing why at every step?

This is the place to which intuitive intelligence can take us. But we are not expected to start here. To build this trust in the Infinite there are initial steps we can take, and the primary step is to understand where intuitive intelligence resides. This is the final piece in understanding the science of intuition.

Intuitive intelligence and the science of the heart

From where does the impulse of intuitive intelligence begin? It is commonly assumed that intuition resides in the third eye – the chakra between our eyes and a little higher in our forehead – connected to our brain's sacred chamber (the pineal and pituitary glands). This is only partially true. Our third eye is the periscope of our intuition – it is not where intuition begins. Intuition is the language of the Infinite. But what is the substance of that one-ness? Love is always the answer. Love is the essence of everything.

Everything that is not love does not exist, as *A Course in Miracles* reminds us. Love is the only eternal and enduring aspect of us and of everything. If that is the case, then, from where do we express and receive love when we are in human form? The heart. And not just our metaphysical heart. It is as accurate to say that our heart chakra (the energy centre at the middle of our chest) and our anatomical heart both form our intuitive intelligence centre. But let's begin with the energy centre, the heart chakra. Our heart chakra at the centre of our chests is the meeting point between our three higher chakras and our three lower chakras. It is the point in our physical and energetic bodies from which we communicate with the world and with the Infinite. The heart is the bridge between human and divine consciousness. The heart, the cosmic heart, is our centre of intuitive knowing and is the home of our nonlocal intuition.

As Meggan Watterson tells us in *Reveal*, it was believed in 15th Century France that "the sixth sense was that of the heart ... the heart as a sense as developed and utilized as our capacity to taste or touch. The heart was understood to be not just an organ but spiritual chamber, a meeting place, a field of inner divinity".[12]

I first heard the following account of the growth of the human embryo from my yoga teacher: when a new life is conceived in utero, something remarkable happens around day seventeen of gestation. Into the primitive kidney bean shape of the new life forming, down the primitive space that will become the throat, a cluster of cells appears from somewhere in the womb. Science does not know from whence these cells come. This small cluster of cells moves into the primitive branches of what will become the lungs and the heartbeat begins. Quite literally, the substance of the heart is a scientific mystery. Its beginnings are of an unknowable origin. The heart is the bridge between the Infinite and the human.

It can speak the language of the body, the language of feelings, and it can also speak the language of the Infinite. We may know this intuitively but there is also incredible science to back up our innate knowing. The heart has the largest electromagnetic field of any part of the human body. What does this mean? At the quantum level, subatomic particles are ripples in an electromagnetic field. The ripples create those fields. So subatomic particles, which are not particles but waves of motion, move in a field. Everything, from the subatomic particle to the entire universe generates a field. We are fields, within fields, within fields. These fields of motion influence everything around us. Our field is influencing the field of the Universe, as well as the field of the person next to us. We know that there is a unified field connecting everything. Our heart is the communication portal to the Infinite field because it generates the largest field of any part of the human body. It is literally the bridge between our local and nonlocal selves.

The anatomical heart contains its own brain, a cluster of around 40,000 neurons, which communicates more information to our head brain than our head brain does to the heart. In a study by HeartMath's psychophysiologist Rollin McCraty in 2004, it was found that a participant's heart rate significantly slowed before a future emotional picture was shown to the participant; that while both the heart and brain receive and respond to intuitive information, the heart appears to receive intuitive information before the brain. When interviewed by Sophy Burnham for her book the Art of Intuition, McCraty went on to say that the heart "appears to play a direct role in the perception of future events .... What our studies suggest is that heart is the main conduit that connects us to our higher self, and that it is the heart that relays intuitive information to the brain".[13]

The key to living in an intuitively intelligent state is what I call Congruence, and HeartMath call Coherence. Gregg Braden refers to it as Resonance. We are incongruent when the logical brain, usually through feelings of fear, ignores or resists the intuition that emerges from the heart brain. Coherence or Congruence is created through generating the feeling states of forgiveness, gratitude, and compassion. When we move into a coherent state, the heart and brain act together. This is exactly what we need to occur to make our intuition clear and accurate. The mind must bow to the intuitive intelligence of the heart. We literally alter our physical form through the emotions we feed our electromagnetic heart (which is 5000 times more electromagnetic than the brain). We alter the electric and magnetic fields of the atom by changing our emotions. The heart is also the portal to the nonlocal – the communication centre between our consciousness and the consciousness of the Infinite is through the heart centre. This is because, as we will go on to learn, feelings are the language of the Universe.

If we want to become the most intuitive version of ourselves, if we want to become conversant in the language of God, then we simply must devote our life to love. We must pray every day that the blocks to love are removed from our heart. This is why activating our intuition is an act of service of the highest order. We are freeing ourselves from fear to become the love from which we were created, and to which we will return. It is possible to live a life without fear. Activating our intuitive intelligence is the way, because an activated intuition is a return to love. Everything I teach about becoming highly intuitive is ultimately, always, about removing the blocks to love. We all have these blocks, and behind them resides our natural, eternal, and unchanging state of being. In this state, intuition is simply not even talked about. There is no need – we are one with all that is. And when we are in this state, we don't need a language to communicate with what we already are. Intuition is the bridge we use to get us to the place where we know we don't need a language. We *are* the language wordlessly speaking itself into every moment of existence. When we are there, the bridge simply falls away. We return to love.

The practice: Heart Congruence

Heart Coherence is a practice developed by HeartMath Institute and is a state in which the brain and heart work to produce a combined effect greater than the sum of their separate parts. Below is a version of the practice of Heart Coherence/Resonance adapted and extended from the HeartMath Institute version.

As discussed, the intelligence of the heart brain exceeds that of the cranial brain, and the heart communicates more information to the cranial brain than the other way around. We move into a state of Heart Congruence when the heart and brain are working in harmony, and it is this state, which allows us to know our intuitive intelligence with ease. It is the bridge between the local and nonlocal. It has many other incredible physiological benefits also, but for now, let us use this practice as preparation for taking the first step on the path of our intuitive intelligence, which is moving beyond simply knowing our intuition to trusting it and acting upon it.

The practice of Heart Congruence is one of the best ways to prepare to access nonlocal intuition. Recalling that it is our "passionately focused attention" that allows nonlocal intuition to activate, we can bring ourselves into the frequency of the Infinite with this same single-focused attention. Even if we do not yet know what it is we want to create, we utilise the same process to get to the one mind, the space where the knowing already exists. Practicing Heart Congruence is a brief, yet disciplined, process.

Here's the process.

- First, close the eyes. Turn your attention inwards, away from the outer world of local reality.
- Extend the breathing to the count of five on the inward breath and five on the out breath. Continue this for a few breaths. Then, Aadjust this to your own comfortable rhythm. The intention is to signify to your nervous system that you are safe, and your physiology can relax.

- Take two fingers or your palm to the centre of your chest and lightly touch this part of your body. Here, we are bringing our consciousness to this part of physiology, inviting our mind to follow.
- Now, turn all your thoughts to the states of compassion, gratitude, appreciation, and care. You can do this most readily in the beginning by making a mental list of all the things for which you feel gratitude from the last 24 hours of your life. No matter how small, the idea is to really feel the feelings of gratitude, compassion, freedom and joy. Allow yourself to enter fully into them without hesitation.
- Let yourself be consumed by these feelings. Do this for at least as 3 minutes (you'll perhaps observe that this feels like a really long time at first!).
- It may feel as though there is a field of energy surrounding your heart area that is expanding the longer you stay in this practice. Imagine, feel or sense that field and notice that sense of expansion.
- Gently lower your hand to your lap and let go of the practice. When you are ready open your eyes and go about your day.

Practice this as often as you can. It prepares you for everything in the best way possible. This can be done with eyes open and without the physical touch if you are in an environment in which it is not comfortable to use these aspects. In fact, the original HeartMath technique is taught in this way so that it can be done anywhere at anytime. My preference is for the eyes closed and the physical touch, but the end aim of this practice is to maintain the congruence at all times.

Your dominant intuition skill

We all have a dominant way of receiving our intuition, or an intuitive skill that we can call *clairs*. These skills include clairaudience (clear hearing), clairvoyance (clear sight), claircognisance (clear knowing), and clairsentience (clear feeling). We each possess the capacity for these intuitive skills, but only one of the four clairs is our dominant – or first – skill. Whilst these are associated with our dominant physical senses, we can think of the clairs as the nonlocal version of our senses. Let me break these down a little more.

Let's begin with clairsentience, for this is my dominant clair. The certainty in my body is how I register when the meaning I am assigning to the feeling of nonlocal intuition is accurate. Very often I feel it as a gentle pressure, which indicates I am ready to speak if I am working with a client, for example. I feel in a state of flow with that feeling state. If I step out of it, perhaps using a word that is not quite accurate, I feel a pulling sensation in my body.

The feeling I receive is the feeling of the nonlocal through my local body, just as the clairvoyant translates the symbolic sight of the nonlocal into usable local information. Clairsentience is perhaps the least understood of the clairs, but also the most common. We can easily confuse what it means to "feel" our intuition. It is important to note that the feeling is not simply energetic sensitivity. Even though I feel the intuited information, it is not literal. I may have a literal sensation in my body, for example a sensation of pain when my client has a backache. But the intuited information is speaking through the nonlocal sense and, as such, I am not in suffering because of that pain, or it may pass in an instant, just enough time to give me the information I need.

The clairaudient hears through her nonlocal hearing sense. In other words, rarely will it be as if there is someone standing next to us whispering to us, although it can happen, and most people have had the experience of this in their lives. More commonly, the intuited information is experienced as language as though the words are being fed nonlocally to the person receiving them. It is an uncommon primary clair, and in most instances the person receives through another clair and then has an almost instant translation into language. This is different to channelling, which I will touch on briefly here. When we channel we open to a nonlocal being speaking through us, using our body as the vehicle. It is, when practiced with care and skill, a profound co-creative experience perhaps most famously embodied in our time by Abraham Hicks. The energy of Abraham, the nonlocal part of the pair, speaks through and with Esther Hicks, the local person inhabiting human form. Channelling, whilst the literal receiving of the voice into you and through you, can still be experienced through anyone of the clairs. When I channel I still experience the clairsentience that is my dominant skill. It guides me to know if I have stepped out of my flow with this energy moving through me.

Clairvoyance is perhaps the most widely referenced of the clairs. For many it is shorthand for all psychic skill. It is a specific way of receiving the nonlocal that uses symbolic sight as the gateway. Intuition is symbolic by nature and so it is the work of the clairvoyant to translate the often-nonliteral imagery perceived through the inner sight into usable information. Infrequently, the sight of the clairvoyant is literal, and they can perceive through the physical sense of vision the colours of the aura for example, or beings who have crossed over, or the site of illness in the body. It is important not to believe that this makes the clairvoyant more powerful. It is far more efficient for nonlocal intuition to be expressed through nonlocal or non-dominant senses. It can be exhilarating to literally see, but if we privilege this kind of clairvoyance we are dismissing the vast power of our nondominant senses.

Claircognisance, in my experience, is usually the domain of men, but not always. This is the knowing that comes with absolute certainty. A thought or an idea "drops in" to the mind and it is instant knowing, even if that thought has no priors. In other words, it is not the work of logic, deduction, or reason. The thought may appear seemingly out of nowhere and the truth of it is experienced instantly, even without evidence. This kind of clair can be associated with acausality, the effect of events being put into motion without seeming cause, or in defiance of the laws of time and space. Nonlinearity is another way to think about how claircognisance operates, or indeed all the clairs. When we stop thinking of time as linear, and instead operate from the reality of oneness then we can truly open into a state of trust and delight in how our intuition is operating.

It is valuable to know our dominant intuitive skill because then the access to the intuition is more natural and easeful. In other words, we receive more readily. We may be good at all these ways of receiving, but in my experience we all still have a dominant skill. In time we notice that intuition is pouring forth into us with such ease that we cannot identify the individual skill it is moving through. It is us in flow with cosmic consciousness, and that is the aim. In the beginning, identifying our dominant and natural way of accessing our intuition is like figuring out if we are left or right-handed. It will come much more easily to us if we use what we are already predisposed to doing. It is like fast-tracking our connection, and so with my intuition students we begin with this process

The practice: identifying your dominant clair

As we are now in a Heart Congruent state, the precursor to all intuitive knowing in the clearest and most expedient form, we are ready to connect to our dominant clair. You may already know this, but I invite you to engage in the practice all the same. We can always deepen our relationship with our intuition, and it is very exciting to do so. It is not a fixed skill and is ever-expanding. I recognise in my own relationship to my intuition that it has evolved to the point that I do not necessarily know which of the senses are being used. It is a state of flow with my intuition. My primary clair is clairsentience. Connecting to this was life-changing for me, because it gave me permission to trust what and how I was intuiting.

We are going to use a guided visualisation to ascertain which of your clairs is dominant. This is a powerful to use at anytime to connect to our higher consciousness, and it works very well for us to become deeply intimate with which clair is guiding us. As you move through the steps, notice how the visualisation appears to you. Do you feel, see, know? When it comes time to request the guidance, be aware of whether you are hearing, seeing, feeling or knowing. You may use this practice as often as you like, and each time you do, you will get more clarity on how the non-local information is appearing to you. This practice is designed to show you your way of receiving your intuition. Intuition is always instant and as you have clear intention to receive you'll instantly "know" what is there for you.

- To begin, make sure you are in a comfortable seated position, and that you won't be disturbed.
- Close your eyes and deepen your breath.
- Let go of all the effort required to bring you to this point in your day.
- Go into Heart Congruence for 3 minutes.
- Feel, sense, think about or imagine a spark of light at the centre of your chest. This may be a sphere of light, or even a flickering flame. Trust what you see, feel or know.
- With every breath in and out, notice the light expanding. The light expands to fill every cell in your heart and chest.
- With every breath in and out, easily and gracefully, the light expands like wild fire, spreading upwards to every cell in your shoulders and down your arms, right to the tips of your fingers.
- Easily, gracefully, the light moves up through your neck and throat, filling every cell with your holy light.
- The light moves up through your skull, and into your brain, right to the top of your head.
- The light moves, easily, downwards now through the trunk of you body, down the front and back of your body, with ease and grace, filling every cell with radiant light.
- The light moves down through your legs, all the way down to your feet and right to the tips of your toes. Easily and gracefully, with every breath, your entire body now illuminated by your radiant light.
- Breathe deeply.
- The light moves outwards now through the limits of your physical body to infuse your subtle anatomy with this holy fire. Your entire energy body bathed in the light of your heart consciousness.
- And still this light expands, effortlessly, easily, expanding outwards to fill the entire space in which you sit.

- With each breath, the light expanding, to fill the entire space and then outwards, across the suburb or region, filling the entire state or county, easily, gracefully, the light of your heart consciousness expanding outwards. No effort required.
- The light continues to expand across continents and oceans, with every breath, until your light encompasses the entire planet.
- See, feel or know yourself now, to be seated on top of the globe, holding the entire planet in your light. The light of your consciousness surrounding the entire planet.
- Breathe deeply.
- In this state of effortless expansion, you are intimately connected with the Field of the One Mind.
- Feel the embrace of the Infinite all around you.
- Now, ask silently or out loud now, *what would you have me know at this time?*
- Await the response to request for support from the Infinite, and trust that intuition is always instant. Let the information come to you in whatever way it will. Intuition is subtle and symbolic. Trust what you hear, feel, see or know. Take as long as you need.
- When you are ready, begin to deepen your breath. Take your hands over your heart centre, and spend a moment in silent gratitude to the infinite intelligence that is always guiding you.
- Bring some gentle movement back to your body, and when you are ready, blink open your eyes.

Now, take up a pen and your journal and note the guidance you received. As you record your experience, pay close attention to how you were receiving your intuition through your nonlocal senses. Did you feel it? Did you see an image or symbol? Did you hear a voice speaking to you, yours or another's? Did you just know what the information was for you?

For example, I often have a feeling and then an immediate knowing at the same time. The feeling is accompanied by a mental certainty. When I see an image or symbol it will be secondary to the feeling of that symbol. Simply put I might *feel* a sense of white flowers and moonlight. As soon as I pay attention to this feeling the mental image appears in glorious detail. There will always be one clair before the others.

It is usually not difficult for us to connect to our intuition. It is enormously difficult though for us to trust what we hear, feel, see or know especially if it goes against our reason. When you become really intimate with your dominant clair you deepen your trust of how your intuition is working through you, and trust in what comes.

This practice is outlined here so you can identify your dominant clair. It is a tool best used for the self and to discern the right action in your own life. Eventually, when the heart congruent state is practiced the intuitive knowing becomes a state of effortless flow. No question even need be asked. In every moment we accept our intuitive guidance even when it goes against the ego mind. The more we practice the more refined the muscle of our intuition becomes.

Intuition is almost always accompanied by a feeling state of certainty. This is how it can be differentiated from the ego. Even when the intuited wisdom brings up fear (because it may be guiding us in new and different directions to the ones we intended), we can know it to be our intuition because of that accompanying feeling of certainty. It takes a great deal of energy to resist that knowing, and yet that is what most people do with their intuitive insights because we are afraid of change.

Intuition comes through the senses, although it is easier to think of these as our inner senses rather than our external senses. Sight, hearing, touch, taste and yes, even smell, can play a role in receiving revealed knowledge. These are not our external senses. They are the senses of and through the soul language that is intuition, so they are subtle and internal.

Reconnection to our sixth sense can be difficult, but it is not difficult in the same way that learning a new language is, because it is not confined to linear time or causality – it is not one piece of information after the next. Nonlocal intuition gives us an unfair advantage because it is acausal. In other words, when we commit to opening to our innate intuitive knowing, we will find that the Infinite conspires to make it so. Communing with the Infinite through our intuition is our natural state. The Infinite wants us connected and plugged in, and so when we set our intention to open to our sixth sense, we will find that our awakening leaps and bounds ever forward. HeartMath Institute states of nonlocal intuition that, "this experience of an immediate, total sense of the thing as a whole is quite unlike the informational processing experience of normal awareness. In normal awareness, the contents of the mind are updated incrementally, as the moment-by-moment sequences of sensory experience unfold."[13]

*

In summary, intuitive intelligence is specifically the development of *nonlocal intuition*, which can be described as the transcendence of our limited human consciousness as we open to Infinite consciousness or the One Mind. We access the information we need with ease and grace in any given moment. Time and space are obsolete in this Infinite consciousness, and this is because of the interconnectedness of everything. Intuition is located in the heart, for the heart is the portal to the Infinite, and our intuitive intelligence increases when we focus on the feeling states of compassion and gratitude. We can get even clearer in our intuition when we identify our dominant way of receiving our intuition. Intuition is innate within us, rudimentary in its survival form, but as we awaken on our spiritual journey our relationship with our intuition evolves. We may even reach the place of divine surrender – visionary intuition – at which time we are willing to hands our lives over to the Infinite one mind, knowing that trust of God so deeply within us that we are holding nothing back. Importantly, it takes congruence between head and heart for us to not just know our intuition, but to trust it and live it, and that is the process of becoming intuitively intelligent.

Chapter 3

The Law Of Mentalism

The mind is very powerful, and never loses its creative force. It never sleeps. Every instant it is creating. It is hard to recognize that thought and belief combine into a power surge that can literally move mountains. It appears at first glance that to believe such power about yourself is arrogant, but that is not the real reason you do not believe it. You prefer to believe that your thoughts cannot exert real influence because you are actually afraid of them.

— *A Course in Miracles*

The three immutable Hermetic laws are as real and meaningful to me as my own breath, because I have witnessed them at work in my life. It takes inner spiritual fierceness to do this, to notice and trust the divine at play in the seeming struggles of our lives. Each law introduced in this book is illustrated by a turning point in my awakening. Spiritual paradox is strongly evident in these personal stories and in the Hermetic laws and, yes, in all spiritual seeking.

What is the spiritual paradox? In the simplest of terms is it this: we are both destined, and we have absolute free will. It is the quality of our choices that determines the quality of our lives, not the choices themselves. It can mean that for great lengths of time it feels we cannot do anything but operate on blind faith. However, when we look to the laws we are suddenly powerfully equipped with a way to expedite that process of accepting the higher purpose of the suffering and bringing our lives into alignment.

The turning points in my life that I share in the following pages, much like the Hermetic teachings, do not reveal their meaning all at once. I had to live through them to understand the gnosis – the divine meaning – held within them. The jewel inside the outer layers of seeming suffering can only be accessed by that (often blind) faith, and a certainty in the sacred laws. The laws give us a means by which to make sense of the apparent inconsistencies of our lives, and to view the events we experience with a universal perspective. This is a vital step in spiritual maturing. It is evidence of spiritual maturity that we do not take everything personally. We learn to make peace with the paradox and in so doing we gain a state of unending grace. This is surrender in action; we are not asked to give up more than we will gain – ever. In the moment, we may not be able to see beyond our suffering to what is on offer. We may not be able to understand that we indeed *created* it, for this is what the first law teaches us. The law of mentalism sounds like a very lofty law, but it is very straightforward. This principle embodies the understanding that everything in the universe is created by thought. There is nothing that exists in the universe where this is not the case. The great law of spiritual psychology is that it is our thought or belief that creates our reality. Everything that exists is energy: matter is just densified energy, energy is just refined matter. All is just energy.

The idea of the holograph is useful here, and many have spoken of the holographic nature of the Universe. I'll keep it simple: in a holographic image, all parts contain the whole. It goes with the law of mentalism. When the law states that all is of the mind, we can conceive of this as both the one mind – or the mind of God if you like – as well as our individual minds. Even now we can glean an inkling of how spiritual paradox is at work here. We are one with the mind of God, and nothing exists that is not. We reside in the mind of the Infinite and everything we live is a projection of that Infinite consciousness. So, why the suffering, we may ask? If we reside in the mind of the benevolent Universe, then how could anything be less than love? Well, herein lies the paradox of spirituality. Within the Infinite one mind we have free will and the choices we make, the beliefs with which we seed our consciousness, are what determines how our personal piece of the Infinite appears. We can live inside the one mind of God and experience a living hell. It is our power to create through our consciousness that makes us what we are – divinity itself and it is our humanness that makes us forget that power, or to use it with such hit and miss results.

Another way to think about it that I have found very useful is to imagine that life is a computer simulation that my consciousness is running. This is not my idea – many have talked about human reality in this way. Whether you take it literally or metaphorically, it offers a way to loosen the ego mind's grip on feeling like a passive receiver of life. If I don't like the simulation I am walking around in, just as with most virtual reality games, I need to upgrade the program. My consciousness is determining the quality of the simulation.

This analogy works so well for me because it reminds me that I am consciousness masquerading as form, and the quality of my consciousness, according to the law, directs the quality of my life. The law states that all is one. We are all connected, we are literally all one. There are no more atoms than were created at the moment of the Big Bang, yet almost all the cells of our physical body are replaced over and over again, some types within just days or weeks, others over months, and years. So, we are literally made up of one another. At the level of science as well as the level of metaphysics, we are all one.

The law of mentalism reminds us that we are pure consciousness before we are matter. Or *energy first, physical second*. We begin as pure potential, as pure consciousness, and we remain that way. But as Caroline Myss tells us, before we descend into human form we drink from the River of Forgetting; if we didn't we would find confining ourselves Infinite into the limited human form intolerable. Instead we use each life as an opportunity to move through a process of reawakening to what and who we are, at deeper and deeper levels (which is love). Each lifetime is an invitation to go deeper, and the very reason we incarnate at all. My reawakening in this lifetime, the beginning of my spiritual adulthood, really took hold in 2001 when I was twenty-four years old, in the days before September 11 changed the world forever.

The first turning point: Leaving home

Archetype: The Maiden
Mantra: I do not have a life, I am life. Eckhart Tolle
Intuition: Survival

August, 2001. I had only just begun to make sense of Rome. I recall coffee bars that were standing room only. The Italians knock back their Caffé Nero in a gulp before moving back onto the street. No ridiculous flavouring or sitting on a cup for hours. Milk in coffee was for morning only and never after a meal. I was captivated by the casual indifference of the Romans towards the tourists. I adored the way the ancient and new, ruins and contemporary cool, were knit together as one. I loved this city even though I had barely begun to scratch the surface, when it all came to a shuddering halt.

There was no Wi-Fi then, I certainly didn't have a mobile phone. I sat next to my boyfriend in a cramped Internet café, calling my parents back in Australia to let them know I had arrived safely on the next leg of my journey. We had begun in London and made our way up to Scotland to take in the rich culture of Edinburgh and the vast beauty of the highlands. I had felt instantly at home. I felt I knew that place. After a few days in Paris we caught an overnight train to Venice and then travelled south through Sienna and Florence, finally arriving in Rome. There was much more planned. I had been dreaming of this adventure for years. After a few more days travelling through Italy I was leaving my boyfriend behind to undertake my first spiritual pilgrimage to the sacred sites of the divine feminine in France. After that, my life would be in London. Or so I thought.

Back in the Internet café in Rome I was frustrated that my mother wouldn't talk to me. She asked me to pass the phone to my boyfriend. His face turned white as he listened to her words. I knew the news was not good. My little sister, only eighteen at the time, had been in a car accident. When my mother finally agreed to speak to me she asked me to come home. Angel had 48 hours to live. I don't really remember much of the next 24 hours, but with the help of the hostel manager I was booked onto the next flight to Brisbane. I was a mess. I left my boyfriend behind and began an epic 36-hour journey to Australia. I sobbed a lot. I can only imagine what my fellow passengers thought. Then, all of sudden, about 8 hours away from my destination I was overtaken by calm. Grace moved through me. I had never experienced anything like it. I knew in that instant that Angel would live. I leaned back in my seat and fell asleep.

I cannot say the rest was easy. It was not. Angel had broken nearly every bone in her body when a car crossed into her lane travelling 100 kilometres an hour on that dark highway in country Queensland. For the first eight days she was in an induced coma. She spent her nineteenth birthday in that state. September 10, 2001. The next morning after her birthday, I awoke in the apartment my brother and I were sharing. He was up before me and as I emerged from the bedroom he pointed to the television. The image of the planes hitting the twin towers repeated in a seemingly unending loop. We sat for hours horrified, mesmerised, by the images on the screen, until it was our turn to go and sit with Angel at the hospital. Our personal family crisis was suddenly writ large. The backdrop to our experience was as surreal as the one we were living and breathing at the hospital. I hadn't formulated a plan for what would happen with my life after Angel was home. It was too soon to be thinking beyond the moment as she lay in a coma in ICU. But after that day, September 11, I knew with certainty I would not be going back to London.

My dominant intuition is clairsentience. This means I feel my intuitive knowing. The certainty I felt that I would not return to London was calm and grounded. This is how I knew I could trust it. What happened after that, however, was akin to panic. What was my life? You see, I hadn't come home to the place where I had grown up, to the job I had always been doing. My sister's accident was on the other side of the country from where I grew up. My sister and my parents had only very recently moved there. We were 5 hours away by plane from my home in Australia, but was that home anymore? I had quit my job, given up my apartment, and said my goodbyes. I was meant to be living in Europe. I wasn't meant to be spending my days in a country hospital in regional Australia, helping nurse my sister back to health. I felt suddenly without an identity. I also knew this was no mistake. After the panic subsided I could see the power in what had been created in the emptiness. I existed only in present time. I had nowhere to be and nothing to do other than be with my baby sister as she learnt to walk again and regain her strength.

I did not yet know why my life had been so powerfully rerouted, but I knew in time it would become clear. I could feel that there was a plan for me and I felt secure in that knowing that everything was being taken care of. Some days. On other days I was angry and frustrated. Yet, there was nothing to do but be what was needed in that extraordinary time. I remember driving back from the hospital late at night through sugar cane fields ablaze with fire. This is how the cane crops are prepared for harvest. Driving the narrow, dark road through fields of black sugar cane and golden cleansing fire felt like a purification ritual for my soul.

Within six months I was living in Melbourne, Australia, beginning a PhD in magical realism, about to meet the man I would marry and who would set my life on yet another path I could never have anticipated. It could not have been any different to what I had imagined my life would look like at that time. I had thought I was going to continue the job I had done up to that time and be a glamorous actor's agent in London living a rock-and-roll lifestyle. Instead, I was immersing myself in the life of a student at one of the greatest universities in the world and living in a share house. Poetically, my first home in Melbourne was near Lygon Street, Melbourne's own little Italy, and I spent many hours sipping my caffè latte outside gorgeous Italian coffee bars. Much to the Roman's horror, I am sure, I always drank mine with latte no matter what the time of day.

How could I know that my sister would not die? How did I know that the best next step for me was to go south to Melbourne instead of north to London? The law of mentalism explains both these events. My consciousness is one with the one mind, just as is my sister's consciousness. When I remember that all is of this one mind, and the quality of that oneness is not fixed matter, but pure nonlocal energy, it is easy to understand how this superhighway of information could transmit this knowing without contact via physical matter. My mind, my consciousness, was entrained on my sister at the exclusion of almost all else. This single and direct focus made it super easy for the one mind to know what it was I wanted to receive information about. When we understand that all is of the one mind, we begin to meet our immense power to know without knowing *how* we know. In other words, non-locally. All that ever was and ever will be is in that oneness. Nothing is outside of it. What cannot be known? This is also a textbook example of survival intuition.

Survival intuition is primal within us. It should be considered mundane in its ordinariness. This does not mean that it is not divine, or that it does not have to be trained. In extreme times such as this experience with my sister, the survival intuition appears to ratchet up several notches, so even the most cynical amongst us cannot miss it. Everyone has a story like this. Our survival – or rudimentary intuition is always on and is always waiting to serve us and make our lives blessedly easeful. For example, most days the outfit that I wear pops into my consciousness before I even get to the closet. Effortless. I put it on and know without needing to know why that it is just the right clothing for me that day. Does this seem too superficial to be on the Infinite's agenda? Why wouldn't it be a matter of course that every decision I make is already available to me even before the question is formed? It is our own judgment that some things are "spiritual" and some things are not that prevents our intuitive knowing from being present in our lives all the time. Likewise, our judgment of ourselves, and of our worthiness permitting us to be (or not) in communion with the Infinite can determine how readily we hear our intuitive knowing. Nothing is not divine. All is of the one mind after all. All is God.

The same goes for my certainty that my life was in Australia rather than Europe after Angel's accident. Was this fear, a knee-jerk reaction to the state of the world and the state of my sister's health? It could easily appear this way, and in many times of my life this would be the truth, but in this case, there were several excellent indicators that it was not my fear limiting me but my higher or non-local consciousness directing me. For one, the knowing came with an absolute certainty. Two, the knowing was instant, I didn't to-and-fro. It was as though the decision had been made for me and in the delicious way of spiritual paradox, it *had* been made for me. The thing is this superhighway, the one mind, is not just a vessel that holds our individual and collective consciousness.

It is, if you like, the only mind. We are simply fragments of that one Infinite mind. So, not only can we connect to one another, as I did with my sister on that long flight from Rome, I can also connect to the eternal part of myself, my soul. My soul is not separate from the mind that created the Universe. It is that mind.

What are any of us doing when we pray for an answer? We are bearing witness to the hope as old as time that something greater than us will answer. What is answering is the one mind, or the God-mind, or the higher part of you. All these ideas are the same. It doesn't matter to me what we call the one mind. What is important to recognise is that we are it, and it is us. Within the Infinite one mind, of which we are a divine piece, we have, for a time, been given an individual piece of that Infinite mind and we are free to do with it what we will. But it is no less perfect, wise, or connected to all time and space, all that ever was and all that ever will be. With this awareness comes great power, and even popular culture can distil this, for as Spiderman tells us, with that power comes great responsibility. Most of us will attempt to abdicate that responsibility.

Our consciousness is the driver – or the commander – of what we draw forth from the one mind. When I knew my life was in Melbourne, was it some power other than me making a choice on my behalf? No, it was my choice and the peace that came with it showed me how it was a choice made in partnership with that one, higher, wiser, pretty much all-knowing mind. The relationship between the one mind and our own individual piece of the one mind is a partnership. The spiritual paradox writ large. I am destined, and I have free will. Making peace with this paradox is the free ride to your best life.

The Subconscious Mind

Our consciousness is made up of multiple parts, although we'll focus on two primarily – the reasoning conscious mind, and the subconscious mind. What we would like to imagine is that the reasoning mind – that part we identify with our personality, our likes, the things by which we define ourselves (*I like jazz, I don't like sushi etc.*), is in charge. Indeed, this part of our consciousness is like the captain of the ship. According to psychologist and author Venice Bloodworth, the relationship between the conscious and subconscious mind is like this: "Every thought that enters the conscious mind is subjected to our reasoning power. If we accept an idea or thought as true, it is then carried forward to the subconscious mind to act on."[14]

The subconscious is beneath the deck, and is the largest part of our consciousness, made up of around 90%–95% of consciousness in most people. Bloodworth offers that the subconscious mind is "the marvellous phase of your mind that brings things into existence by the sheer power of thought". The subconscious mind is highly programmable, and because we have mostly not been aware that we are one with the mind of the Infinite, we have believed our fear stories, and the fear stories of the world around us, and we have focussed our attention on those things, without any filter. The captain of the ship has looked this way and that, absorbed by the events of life, and passed these very mixed instructions to the subconscious below deck. The result is that the bulk of our consciousness is attuned to the negative, fear-based dominant consciousness of the collective reality we witness. We have forgotten that we are in a co-creative relationship with the one mind. Our access to the one mind gets blocked because our subconscious is full of stuff we didn't even know we chose to focus on. The result of this for our lives is chaos. Most of us live with a general sense of managed chaos waiting for the next event or emotional storm to derail us. This is because if the mind is uninvestigated, if we have not taken the time to explore the contents below deck, then we cannot know the difference between our fear and our intuition.

There is another vital function of the subconscious beyond its role as the storehouse of whatever our consciousness is entrained upon. It is also the entry point to the one mind of the Infinite. If we want to meet our Infinite, unlimited selves, then we need to clear out the fear that inhabits the subconscious mind. Think of it this way: the subconscious is a basement full of boxes of fear. The boxes are piled so high that we think that all that exists down here is darkness and fear. As we start to meet our fear and make some precious space, we notice a door on the back wall that we previously couldn't even see. This door becomes clearer and clearer as we meet and clear more and more fear, until one day we can read the sign upon the door that reads: "Here stands the gates to the Infinite. All are welcome." As Bloodworth also offers, the subconscious mind is:

The spiritual part of us, and through it we are connected with the Divine and brought into relation with Infinite constructive forces of the Universe ... part of the Universal Mind and has Infinite resources at its command. Dr Jung tells us that the subconscious mind not only contains all the classified data gathered during all the past life of the individual, but that it contains also all the wisdom of all the immeasurable ages past, and that by drawing upon its power the individual may possess the good things of life in great abundance[15].

Quite literally, the unmet crap below deck blocks the voice of the one mind. What do we do with this? We know we are one with the Infinite mind, and that Infinite intelligence is guiding us. We also now know that we are blocked in receiving that knowing and co-creating our lives because of this very large, very unconscious part of our consciousness. What we do is this: we go meet our fear – so let's go.

Spiritual Self-Esteem

When I began teaching people how to activate their intuitive intelligence, I struggled to know how to put everything I had discovered over twenty years into a process that could be followed step-by-step. I struggled, not because I don't have a process – I do, and it is outlined in replicable detail in this book. I struggled because I was starting at the wrong place. Intuitive intelligence isn't the techniques we use to activate it. To open to our intuitive intelligence, we need to radically shift our belief about ourselves and our true nature. What I have come to know is that the process of activating intuitive intelligence in anyone begins with identifying the primary belief that he or she has about the world. Intuitive intelligence, more than anything else, is the cultivation of the right-minded belief, because as we understand from the law of mentalism, all is of the mind. Only consciousness exists. If the belief necessary for intuitive intelligence is lacking, then I know exactly where to begin with my client.

I have yet to meet a person who is actively living this belief, even if they know it to be true. Knowledge and experience are two very different things. Just as we know it is possible to speak French, it doesn't mean that we will ever take the time to do so. We can believe something to be true but until we put in the work to have a direct experience of that knowing it is purely conceptual, and it cannot alter us.

The belief, or mindset, in which intuitive intelligence flourishes, is this:

> *I am a divine piece of a benevolent God that is always working on my behalf and is communicating with me all the time.*

We need to traverse the divide between knowing that *all is one*, to experiencing that oneness. In other words, to be intuitively intelligent we need to make friends with our divine nature. Intuitive intelligence is a spiritual path. We are all intuitive, powerfully intuitive. We are so powerful in our intuition that in every moment of our lives we can know the right action and be lovingly guided towards our highest truth. It is also true that the human journey is one of forgetting our own inherent nature, and so we must work to activate our connection to our intuitive intelligence. This goes for most of us, but not all. We have all heard of, or perhaps even met, those rare individuals for whom accessing intuition is both highly pronounced and seemingly effortless. And yet even for those who are born with the window wide open to their intuitive powers, the capacity to deepen their intuition is possible. It is in fact the work of this life, for all of us. This is because, as Sophy Burnham tells, becoming more intuitive is exactly the same as becoming more spiritual:

> *When individuals asked Edgar Cayce how to become more psychic, he answered that the goal is simply to become more spiritual, "for psychic is of the soul", he said, and as you become more spiritual, the abilities*

develop naturally. If this individual is not interested in spiritual betterment, he should leave the skills alone.[16]

When we begin to understand this, we crave the activation of our intuitive intelligence in the deepest parts of ourselves. We know that to be disconnected from our intuitive intelligence is to be a somnambulist, sleepwalking in our own life. We know that until intuitive intelligence is awake and alert in our heart and our soul, our minds will always be attempting to imprison us in a palace of fear. We understand that intuition is simply a symptom of an evolving consciousness. And that is what we are all here to do – evolve. The essential requirement for the activation of intuitive intelligence for anyone is thus *spiritual self-esteem.* Intuitive intelligence and spiritual self-esteem are one and the same, for one cannot exist without the other. And they have a symbiotic relationship: one does not come *before* the other, but *because* of the other. You cannot increase your spiritual self-esteem without igniting your intuition, and vice versa.

Intuitive intelligence feels like freedom. It is the state in which we are in total non-judgment, radical acceptance, and feel effortless power. It is the state in which we know we are masters of our waking life, and it is the state of total surrender. It is the recognition that not a single experience in our lives, even our own death, can alter our divine perfection. This is also spiritual self-esteem. It doesn't matter if it is a curiosity in awakening your sixth sense that activates your spiritual self-esteem, or if you discover the innate superpower of your sixth sense in your quest to think better of yourself and take better care of your well-being – either way, they will be attained as one. That's why so many people who start on the health and wellness path end up having a spiritual awakening. The soul is attuned to awakening, and it will take any opportunity it gets to wake us up.

Interestingly, it is possible for people to activate psychic skill and not awaken (just as people can jump on health kicks and never get into spiritual ideas). It is a strangeness to me, as Edgar Cayce's belief earlier suggests, that the acquisition of psychic skill, something done for others perhaps via readings, can come without spiritual awakening. But here's the thing: intuition on its own doesn't take us far enough. Intuitive intelligence is required to make intuition a living thing for our own lives, rather than a trick of the trade for readers.

Here's another thing about this: Intuitive intelligence will no doubt make you more attuned to others – all is one, after all. But intuitive intelligence is about *personal* power. That's the hallmark of spiritual self-esteem. We do not look outside of ourselves for the information we believe is lacking and cannot be accessed ourselves. We might seek support to remove our fear blocks that prevent us knowing our worth, but we do not give away our power.

Intuitive intelligence is waking up to our inherent worthiness. How can this not be so when we look to the Hermetic laws and we are reminded we are one with the Infinite? We have a lot of blocks between us and that fearless state of oneness. Intuitive intelligence is our natural state. It is the state into which we are born, yet everything that happens in our life obscures this natural fearless state. Fearful beliefs layer up on one another every moment of every day, and we move further and further away from the memory of our true nature. The law of mentalism tells us that all is of the one mind. We are not simply made up of that Infinite mind but are in fact one with that mind. We know that the substance of the one mind is love. We know this because we know that nothing, but love exists. What happens in the course of our lives is that we move into fear and away from love, into a belief in our separateness and isolation.

Yet, from the moment that the Universe exploded into being in a blinding flash of light, everything needed to make us was created – nothing new has been added to the mix that makes the building blocks of every atom. We are literally all we ever were, and all we ever will be, right now. The benevolent Infinite, of which we are a divine piece, sends us forth into physical form equipped with everything we need now and forever. We have not been abandoned on a cold and unforgiving planet without meaning and purpose. The Infinite sends us forth and yet we stay intimately connected. In that lies the essence of the relationship between spiritual self-esteem and intuitive intelligence.

Knowing that we are the Infinite and the Infinite is us, and that we have not been forgotten, it is easy to recognise that we are totally and utterly supported throughout our lives in this kind embrace. The Infinite holds us close and whispers to us constantly all that we need to know in every moment. It is clear, then, that our fearlessness, and as such our intuitive intelligence, is not about adding anything to who or what we are. It is not about gaining courage, strength, or bravery, or qualifications, money, or power, or anything else at all – it is about clearing out the blocks to your memory of our truth. That is why when we learn to connect to our intuitive intelligence we are reconnecting to our natural fearless state, and we do this by removing our blocks to our memory of this. It is that simple.

It is also why when I teach people how to become profoundly intuitive, we must begin by meeting our fear.

The Practice: increase your power to serve

When we stop relying on our own readiness to meet our fear and connect to our unlimited selves, then we are much more able to get on with it. This practice is our reminder that the greatest power we have is to know our power is God's power. The best way to increase our power to know ourselves as God is to devote our lives to something greater than our selves, through sacred serve. The most powerful question in the world is, *how may I be of service?*

This is the beginning of true fearlessness. It is the beginning of true power. We do not attain true power when we are simply attempting to gain more for ourselves, for it is breaking the law. When I increase my power I increase the power of all. I must be aware of this or else I strangle the flow of God's power to me by attempting to attain it for a false reality - the illusion that the dream is real and I can hold something for myself that I keep from my brother or sister.

Recite this prayer. For me this is often repeated a hundred times a day:

Dear God, increase my power to serve. And so it is. And it is so.

This is true fearlessness for it is connecting us to our true source of power, which is the Infinite God consciousness.

What's fear(lessness) got to do with it?

When we commit to the path of intuitive intelligence it is possible to live a fearless life. I know this because it has happened for me. Late one night, several years ago, I sat up in my bed unable to sleep. Adrenaline was racing through my bloodstream. I was feeling fear of failure, although it hardly matters what the fear was, as all fear has the same impact. It causes restriction and dis-ease in the body and soul and needs to be cleared out. The other thing to note, is that it has become very easy for me to recognise the fear that I am feeling in any given moment because I have trained myself to do so through all the practices I share in this book. I could almost instantly recognise the deeper meaning of my anxiety and agitation. The fear of failure is an archetypal fear for me, which means that it is part of my purpose in this life to meet and clear it.

I was in the early stages of establishing the Institute for Intuitive Intelligence, and fear of failure was coming up a lot for me. Previously, I would have tried to ignore or rationalise the fear and pushed it down out of my immediate consciousness. That wouldn't work of course. It is never possible to ignore our feeling state – never. Instead, for me, this fear would burst out of me at some inappropriate moment as anger. That was my pattern whenever I tried to ignore what I was feeling.

For the first time in my life, though, on that night, I was ready to awaken to this pattern in me. I was committed with my whole heart to bring light to the dark and to clear out the fear, consciously and presently. As I tuned into the fear coursing through me I moved to meet it. I could feel how it sat in the back of my body and was being fed stressful impulses from events and feelings I had experienced in the past. The fear had nothing to do with the moment. In that moment I was safely tucked up in my bed in my beautiful home, planning a sold-out training program for a group of amazing people. Everything I needed to feel successful and peaceful was in place and yet I was still gripped by fear.

I was drawn into meditation. I scanned my intuition for the best technique to tackle the fear and I recalled a very physical form of meditation designed to powerfully change our state of being. In this meditation, we are up on our feet, arms up in the air, body moving. The mind cannot take control in this form of meditation. It is also a powerful emotional detoxer, and I have had some incredible results with it. That night I jumped straight into the practice. Within minutes I was feeling very clear and light, fully present in the now moment, and attuned to my intuition. These qualities – light, clear, present, intuitive – are the best way to describe what it is to be fearless.

Within an hour of feeling the initial rush of fear, I was free. It was in that moment that I realised the power was in my hands. I recognised that I had so many similar tools with which to face my fear head-on, and to clear it. I knew for the first time that I could live my whole life in this way. In a way that was the night the Institute was truly born, for a fire was lit in my belly and I knew without a doubt that sharing this truth was what I was here to do.

The practice: the Yes Meditation

This is not a quiet or still meditation practice. In fact there is no limit to how physical or embodied we can get with this practice. But let me explain first what we are going to do. We are going to use the understanding that fear is a friendly ally, and that we can alter our response to it.

Fear primes us to say no to our lives. We're saying no to the miracle. We're saying no to opportunities. We're saying no to stepping outside of our fear, and we keep ourselves limited, small and perpetuating the familiar habits of our lives. I want to live an unlimited life and it's entirely possible for us all to do this. We need simply to be unafraid to face our fear.

The word we're going to repeat again and again and again is YES, YES, YES. How that yes expresses itself is entirely up to the individual. We may find that we repeat the yes as a whisper, or a roar, or a kind of a melodious chant, or discordantly, or dancing around the room, it doesn't really matter at all. The power is in saying yes, which is a word that holds a higher frequency than 'no'. Our 'yes' is awakening us to the potential of what we are instead of the 'no' which is constantly shutting us down and keeping us separate, keeping us limited, keeping us 'safe' according to the ego.

There are times when our no to the world is a yes to ourselves, so I am not encouraging us to go out and say yes to everything we are invited to do. This practice is a totally different idea with a very intentional purpose.

In this practice, we are saying yes to ourselves.

The power of this meditation is so potent that I want to invite you to move beyond any feelings of self-consciousness or doubt and simply go into the practice with a curious heart.

- So let's begin, standing or seated.
- Make sure that you are somewhere safe and comfortable and you won't be disturbed. You will be verbalizing out loud so you want to make sure that no one's going to come running in and wondering if something's wrong.
- Close the eyes or keep them open depending on how you are feeling, and if you start moving.
- Deepen your breath. Take a deep breath in through the nose, let it go out through the mouth with a sigh. Let go of all the effort required to bring you to this point in your day.
- Begin repeating out loud the word 'yes', at any pace, any volume. This will change as you go along.

- Hold your arms up in a Y shape that confirms the yes. Holding up your arms in this shape allows you to receive in a very active and symbolic way from the Infinite. You may get tingles in your hands, you might start to feel heat in your body, you might start to feel that sensation of the Infinite reaching out to you at the same time as you reach out to it.
- At anytime, if your body feels to move, then get up and move.
- Simply keep repeating yes, exactly as you feel to do so. Yes. Yes. Yes. Yes. Yes. Yes. Yes. Yes. Yes. Yes. Yes. Yes. Yes. Yes. Yes. Yes. Yes. Yes. Yes. Yes. Yes. Yes. Yes. Yes. Yes. Yes. Yes. Yes. Yes. Yes. Yes. Yes. Yes. Yes. Yes. Yes. Yes. Yes. Yes. Yes. Yes. Yes. Yes. Yes. Yes. Yes. Yes. Yes.
- Continue for as long as you desire.
- When you feel you have reached the end of this meditation, lower your hands to prayer position over your heart.
- Bow your head now to that magnificent, glorious expanded feeling state.
- Feel that expansion, that invigoration, that higher frequency that is actually your true nature.
- When you're ready, bring some gentle movement back to your body. Blink open your eyes. Repeat this as often as you desire.

We are rewiring the subconscious mind by eliminating fear without needing to be cognisant of that fear. We are saying yes to ourselves, and altering our response to fear when it rises. Do this practice as often as it calls you. I notice that the physical aspect of it becomes easier for me each time. It is not something I am called to use often, but when I meet something that I simply cannot surrender to, this practice always serves me so well.

How fear works

I think of the work I do in service to others is as being a fear hunter. Perhaps this is not something normally associated with a lightworker, or intuitive, but the truth is that the two dark and light, fear and love – are intimately connected, so intimately connected that they are one. A more accurate description of what I do would be "absence of love" hunter, but it doesn't roll off the tongue quite so well. The truth is that there is no fear. There is no darkness. These things simply do not exist, except at the level of the dream. When we accept this truth, we begin to perceive not fear and darkness, but instead the absence of those things. It is very hard to see in the dark. Fear likewise constricts we avoid small dark places, they terrify us the most. We imagine, constantly, what might fill those crevices and cracks. We imagine so much fear that we will do everything in our power to avoid looking. We are really doing everything in our *powerlessness*. To avoid ever having to look into the darkness we give away our power to addictions, emotional chaos, and other people. We become so paralysed by this imaginary place that in our minds it becomes a vast cavern, rather than small insignificant pocket of fear that just wants our attention.

Fear is a messenger. It is showing us where there is a faulty imbalance causing restriction and contraction away from the light. It yearns to be brought back into balance, this is nature's desire in everything, and instead we run from the message. We believe the fear, we believe it is real and immutable. We believe fear is our burden to carry, and as such we find flimsy ways to circumvent it – alcohol, drugs, other people's business, picking fights with our partner. These are all strategies employed (and oh, so many more) to avoid the message.

We do have another strategy to avoid meeting and releasing our fear. It is a paradox, but it works incredibly well all the same. Marianne Williamson beautifully articulates it when she states that we tend to become too enamoured with our fear and seduced by its complexities.[17] What does this mean exactly? Let's say we do summon our courage and go and meet our fear. So far, so good. Only love is real, so we're only really going to meet a tiny, tiny speck of love after all. Fear is a messenger. It is showing up in our life because it has a message, and the message is always the same: "*You, dear one, have forgotten your true nature, which is love, and it is now time to return love to where it is restricted or absent.*" What happens over time, though, is that the fear starts to believe in its realness. It has been left alone to stew for such a long time that it has become rooted to its hiding spot. It has made a home there and it has had a lot of time to embellish itself. It has collected data from the events of our lives to legitimise itself. It is insidious where once it was useful. This is what happens when we ignore fear.

And so, we go, ready and willing to meet this old fear. For whatever reason – new love perhaps, or the loss of something we cherished – we have finally been awoken to this fear in us, and how it has motivated or controlled our actions. We finally have enough motivation, albeit external, to look within. Let's say in this case it is new love. Our new partner encourages us to look at how our unmet fear about our overly controlling parent is limiting the amount of love available to them. Well, we don't want that! We love this new boyfriend or girlfriend and we don't want them to leave like so many before them have. We head into therapy or self-help manuals and we go meet that ancient, rooted fear. It looks horribly sad. It has a terrible story of woe, many in fact. It has so many angles to be looked at. It is a truly complex fear: it began with the parent, but so many people have gone on to treat us in the same way. We need to consider all these past relationships. Looked at from another angle, we can see that it wasn't just the controlling nature of our parent, but also the withholding of affection that caused so much suffering. Look again, and we can see it was the absence of the other parent that really created the fear. Not physically absent, but emotionally absent, and after all, isn't that worse? The weight of all this complexity, the back-story to the fear, is deadening. We feel paralysed before it, and not even our new beau's love is enough to pull us out. There is so much rich emotion here that our emotional needs are being met by it, or so it seems. We don't need love when we have this. Most importantly, we now have cause. We have genuine, legitimate evidence for why we can't be happy, succeed, find love, lose weight, and so on and so on. All the time, the cause of our fear is embellished in detail and difficulty, so the roots of the fear deepen into us, and eventually we discern no difference between our fear and us. We are it. We simply find workarounds to avoid releasing it: we choose partners who confirm our unworthiness. We stay unhealthy to confirm our un-lovability. We stay in jobs we loathe to confirm that another person miserably controls our life. And most importantly, we do this all just below the surface. Presented with the evidence, most reasonable people would agree that this is a ridiculous state of affairs. But the consciousness that is operating this fear show doesn't do so on the superficial level. Instead, it is our subconscious mind that reigns supreme here, and it is almost entirely invisible to us.

How then, with a fear that is not real, yet growing every moment into a self-obsessed despot – unmet as it has been for so long, rooted into a level of our consciousness we cannot access – is it possible for us to alter this seemingly inevitable path? Well, that is simple. We must look to the meaning, not the cause.

The practice: what informs our choices?

This practice is powerfully simple. It is an on-the-go, guerrilla-style tool we can use in the moment to bring us back to our intuitive intelligence. What happens in our day-to-day lives, when we have forgotten our true nature, is that we get very caught up in a fear about making the right or wrong decision. For some of us this is immobilising. What if we get it wrong? Whatever it is, we get trapped in our logic and lose our capacity to intuit, to be guided. People often want an intuitive reader to tell them the answer to the myriad of choices before them because they are immobilised by the fear of making the wrong choice. They would rather abdicate responsibility for their lives than risk getting it wrong. Worse, people actually believe that there is a right and wrong choice. We must remind ourselves of the spiritual paradox here.

We are divinely fated and we have absolute free will. Ultimately, we are on this planet for one purpose only, and that is to awaken. So, in truth we cannot make a wrong decision. The soul's purpose – and the Infinite consciousness of which our soul is a part – will always bring us back to where we can most effectively awaken. The Infinite acts non-judgmentally, and in accordance with the law. We need to remind ourselves also here that we can awaken through suffering or joy. God's love for us is totally impartial and

100% unconditional. God gives us what we are calling forth, and will utilise those conditions for the sole purpose of awakening, which determines the quality of the ride of this thing called life.

Here's the practice: Whenever a choice has to be made, ask yourself:

Is my choice one of love or one of fear?

This question is an instant stress relief when we utilise it often enough. By this, I simply mean that we need to get very comfortable with being honest with ourselves about what motivates us. If we are experiencing low self-esteem, the need to be liked and approved of will override our capacity to know if a choice is for love or fear. We might think it is a loving choice to keep going out of our way for a friend who doesn't seem to consider our feelings at all. Even though we might feel put upon and downtrodden by this person, we can't imagine saying no to them for fear of being rejected. Our self-esteem simply couldn't handle it. This is often the case in clients of mine who are trapped in their martyrdom archetype. They keep putting *themselves* in the downtrodden position to confirm their feelings about themselves, and then state that the world couldn't manage without them.

The choice to behave in this way isn't self-loving or loving to the other. When we recall that *all is one,* we are reminded that we cannot do for others what we are not prepared to do for ourselves. We cannot give and give and give to others and never give to the self without breaking the law.

Likewise, deciding to ignore or neglect others, and claiming it as an act of self-love, is not going to fly. The Infinite has a bullshit detector like you wouldn't believe. When we practice all the techniques in this book, we know ourselves too well to fake it. Another great example of fear masquerading as love is what I call *false abundance*. This is when we spend money we don't have on things we don't need in a vain attempt to make ourselves feel better and claim that "God will provide!" This kind of retail-therapy-spirituality is absolutely inauthentic. We are simply being irresponsible and locating our self-worth outside of ourselves. Does that ever work? The answer to that should be pretty obvious. So, we need to ask ourselves, really deepen into the feeling: is this love or is this fear? Like all the tools in this book, this practice will serve as an accurate barometer if we are actively meeting and clearing the fear in our subconscious.

Meaning versus cause

Fear is a messenger. When I began following my path of service I called myself a psychic reader, a word I love because it means "of the soul", and I worked out of a tiny room in a new age shop in Melbourne. I asked my clients to bring me their questions, because I quickly worked out that the information I wanted to give them was often very different to what they wanted to know. The Infinite consciousness working through me wanted to talk to their soul, yet my clients most often wanted to talk about their boyfriends. Most people seek out a psychic reading when something has gone wrong in their lives, and so they come seeking some kind of permission slip from an external authority: permission to leave a marriage, permission to stay with someone who is treating them badly, permission to go against their own inner authority. Most of us are not confused about what to do when the time for action comes, most of us are simply too terrified to do it. That incongruence between head and heart causes fear. It causes anxiety, panic, stress, and disease. We know what our heart is calling us to do, and because it means some kind of external change we pretend we don't know and we suffer for it. My clients in those days didn't want me to talk about quantum physics and why the choice they made literally didn't matter because the meaning of their lives had nothing to do with who they were married to or where they worked. I could not talk about meaning much at all, for most people were interested only in the cause.

One day a beautiful young woman came to see me. She was very distressed because she believed her husband was cheating on her, and she wanted me to find proof. She asked her questions with a steadiness that belied her inner rage. She was waiting to pounce at the first hint of his indiscretion. She needed evidence, so she could trust her own inner knowing. I felt deep compassion for her suffering, but not for the question of whether or not her husband was cheating. The suffering I pitied in her was that caused by the amount of anger she had to generate in order to ignore her own voice. As she sought out the details of *Was he? When? With who?* – all questions I could not and would not be drawn on – I asked her to look to the meaning of this fear in her own life. Most of us don't want to look at our fear. Mostly we will submerge it as deeply as we can and externalise our feelings. In this case, the young woman's fixation on her husband's possible infidelity allowed her to ignore or project her deep fears of unworthiness and self-loathing.

I knew I wasn't a shop psychic, but I didn't know at that time that I was a fear hunter. My clients wanted, for the most part, to abdicate responsibility for their lives. I had one client come four or five times to try to confirm which real estate agent she should use to sell her house. Her confusion was not about which agent to use – she did not want to sell, but her boyfriend was pushing her to do so. She obsessed about finding the right agent as a way to conceal the fear she felt. She was going against her intuitive knowing. She needed to generate emotional chaos in order to try and conceal her intuition. Eventually I told her I couldn't help her. She wouldn't give up the manipulative boyfriend, so great was her fear of being alone. Her life was incongruent.

Occasionally, the possibility of supporting people to become fearless would happen, just often enough to keep me going with what was becoming increasingly frustrating work. I recall another young woman who was bemoaning not having what she wanted – not the right job, not the right partner – and how it all was someone else's fault. I took out a worksheet for The Work, Byron Katie's incredible and simple process for becoming fearless. I asked this young woman if she would be willing to try it, to really investigate how the fear she had for her life was simply a messenger, and she agreed.

As we worked through a specific limiting belief, one that is focused on an external person – in this case her father – I could see something shifting in her. As she wrestled with the belief that her father limited her and controlled her, and that was why she didn't have the life she wanted, something bigger, a truth more powerful than the fear, was emerging. She was excellent at this process, investigating the four questions and the turnaround with courage, peeling back the layers until she could see through the story. Eventually, she stopped and looked at me, saying with sincerity: "If I keep doing this, I have nowhere to hide." I wanted to high-five her! For the first time in my work, a client was sitting before me who was willing to see that the power was squarely in her hands. She was altered. I never saw her again; that is the nature of working as a shop psychic. I do not know if she was able to hold on to that moment of personal awakening and to see the deeper meaning of her struggles, but I know the very real possibility was birthed in her that day.

Eventually, my focus moved from readings to teaching. My mission from that day to this is to activate the intuitive intelligence that resides within each of us. In the client-reader scenario, that was never going to happen. The power imbalance would always make it difficult for the client to step into her truth. My time as a psychic reader in a shop was an incredible training ground, allowing me to deepen into my intuitive power in some of the most challenging situations. I had to be so powerfully in sync with the divine in that place, otherwise the fears and heartaches of my clients would have consumed me. I had to stay in the place of total trust that the divine was working on their behalf, even when they believed their world was falling apart. It is akin to the yoga teacher in training who must accrue a certain number of hours to become qualified. This apprenticeship in witnessing fear on behalf of my clients was a unique and humbling opportunity. As I accrued my hours and gained my experience I also received a masterclass in the techniques the ego mind will use to conceal our fear from us. I understood the problem of this work is when we believe others know more about us than we do. But I also saw the incredible resistance people have in meeting their own Infinite nature. Something had to change, both about the way I was working, and more generally in this unregulated industry. When I closed this first chapter of my work as an intuitive I did not so much walk from it as run. I was at my limit, and I didn't yet know how to change the conversation about intuition. I had not yet birthed the intuitive intelligence method, but the seeds had been sown, and my true path of service had begun.

Ultimately, life is about embracing all of ourselves including our fear, and not being afraid of the feelings of hurt. We hide from our fear in our ego masquerading as pride, or rage, or victimhood, or self-pity, or any combination of those. Acceptance of what is, as we will go on to see, is not the same as sitting down with those who have hurt you and letting them do it again. It is understanding that no matter the events of our lives, it is the stories we tell ourselves about them that causes the suffering.

The law of mentalism has shown us how everything is of the one mind of the Infinite. We are not separate from that one mind. We create our lives from the Infinite consciousness of which we are all a divine part. Yet our unmet subconscious fear can turn our lives into a prison of our own making if we let it. It doesn't really matter how we became fearful, or how long it has been there. What matters is the meaning of that fear. The fear is a messenger guiding us back to the truth that the substance of the one mind is love. Where there is fear, we have simply forgotten our true nature. To awaken is to remember what is real and what is not, and to return to love. To really do this we must overcome our fear that we are not worthy of being what we are, which is God. We must reclaim our spiritual self-esteem. Meeting our unchecked fear is the very best first step on this path.

Chapter 4

The Law of Correspondence

As above, so below; as below, so above.

The second law is the law of correspondence. What the law of correspondence means is that the thoughts and images that we hold in our conscious and subconscious mind will manifest their exact likeness in our external reality. The outer world is a reflection of what is within us. This law, like all the cosmic laws, is impartial, and works unceasingly for the good or the bad. The law of correspondence requires that we know we are in partnership with the Infinite, or God. In other words, we are not doing it alone. This requires absolute trust. For the law of correspondence to really come into right action and to work in our favour, we must possess self-esteem. This is why we began the process of activating our self-esteem in the previous section, we are going to need our spiritual self-esteem.

Why does this law require we trust the Infinite? And what does that have to do with self-esteem?

Let's break it down: the law states that what we hold in our consciousness (remembering that, as the law of mentalism tells us, consciousness is *everything* because all is of the mind) we will manifest in the outer world. This makes sense when we apply it to the law of correspondence, because this law tells us that the inner and outer are in fact one. The trust we need to feel in our co-creative partner, the Infinite, is simply trust in ourselves, because *we are that* – we are God. Trusting the Infinite is one condition of adhering to the law of correspondence.

Then there is the other, often much more tricky condition, tricky especially for spiritual seekers. Conceptually, we can say: "*I trust God.*" We are prepared to believe that the Infinite has our back. We even potentially want to remember that we *are* God. But until we have met our fears of unworthiness, then we cannot truly partner with what we are, with our Infinite nature. We are paying lip service to the idea, and in reality, remain sitting in fear. *As within, so without* is another way of thinking about this law. We cannot say that we believe that the Infinite is all-powerful and then deny that *we are that power* – it's breaking the law. The law of correspondence basically brings us to the inevitable truth that we are divine beings having a finite human experience. We will suffer whilst we believe that we are a limited, human consciousness, because our true nature is trying to cor-respond, or communicate with itself through this experience called life, and our human fear is thwarting those attempts. When we can forgo our limited belief, we begin to see our lives flourish, because the truth of what we are can communicate clearly with itself on all planes, within and without, above and below.

I often quote the Spiderman movies in my workshops: *with great power comes great responsibility*. We think we want to be in possession of our self-worth, but with that worthiness comes the responsibility for our Infinite power. More often than not we run from our own power, thinking everyone else is responsible for the state of our lives, or is better than us, or didn't have the experiences we had and therefore can shine. The responsibility of being all-powerful means that we must ultimately surrender our human frailty. We have to trust that our lives have not gone astray and, most importantly, we must stop blaming God for what has happened to us or what we see around us in the world. We must surrender our fear that we are not God. Or we must surrender our fear that we *are* God. The brilliant and sneaky ego has a million stories to keep us playing small. If we want to save the world we simply must surrender our fear and go meet ourselves as the Infinite. *As within, so without.*

As above, so below begins to make more sense, too, as we start to recover our self-esteem and personal power, which is Infinite power. What does this statement mean? It means that the contents of heaven can be ours on earth in an instant if we are willing to follow this law. How can it be possible to have heaven on earth? Well, once again, by reminding ourselves of the first law, *all is one*, we can see how heaven is not another time and place. It is here in the always, already present. What permits that state of bliss known as heaven to be the reality of our lives? The law of correspondence has the answer, and by now it should be very familiar. Self-esteem. To know ourselves as God, or the Infinite is the bliss of heaven on earth. How can it not be? To remember our true nature is the end of our suffering. It is undoubtedly the cornerstone of spiritual fierceness and intuitive intelligence.

The Law of Correspondence as a communication hotline

Intuitive intelligence, as has been said, is simply a symptom of a healed mind. The healing that takes place when we activate our intuitive intelligence corrects the false belief in separation and removes the blocks to our knowing that we are in partnership with the Infinite. The Infinite contains everything within it. It stands to reason that if we are connected and communicating with the Infinite that *is* all, then we have it all. Not only that, we have the means by which to draw it to us. An activated intuitive intelligence is the most powerful manifestation tool we have. We draw towards us what corresponds to us. Another way to think about the law of correspondence is in terms of *communication*. What conversation am I having with myself and with the Infinite? Am I telling myself the world is a scary place full of dangerous people? Am I telling myself that I am worthless, nothing, weak and vulnerable? That communication is a direct command to the Infinite, and because we are the Infinite, the communication hotline is clear and strong. We are speaking (or thinking or feeling) our fears into reality. The communication is always happening, and as we understand from the levels of mind, it is most often subconsciously calling the Infinite into action. The Infinite corresponds to the communication because we are that powerful. So how do we heal this faulty feedback loop? That's what this chapter is all about. The power of knowing ourselves, and in particular the contents of our subconscious mind, is the most important step to living in accordance with this law.

As *A Course in Miracles* states in Chapter 11 of the text:

You see what you expect, and you expect what you have invited. Your perception is the result of your invitation, coming to you as you sent for it. Whose manifestations would you see? Of whose presence would you be convinced? For you will believe in what you manifest, and as you look out, so will you see in.

It is vital for us to wrap our heads around the idea of correspondence as *communication*. The Infinite doesn't simply correspond to our belief about it. It does it with direct intent. It does it, so we can overcome the faulty belief in separation. Our true nature is Infinite and all-powerful, and anything in our lives that doesn't reflect that is an imbalance that will keep revisiting us until we correct it. It is a communication loop that is designed to bring us back into correspondence with our true nature. God isn't testing us – it is totally impartial. But everything in our lives, within and without, works to support our awakening, so that when we have forgotten, the events we create from that forgetting will bring us home to ourselves.

Can I believe that the Infinite is all powerful, and that it is my partner, and sit in feelings of low self-worth? No. We are breaking the law. The Universe will behave in accordance with our belief. As within, so without. In this case, life will seem like a living hell and God will appear to be punishing or testing us at every turn. As we know that this is simply not possible in truth, we must look to ourselves. How can we heal the belief in separation, the dualism that makes us think that God's power is separate from us, and heaven is a place we can only access when we die? Living intuitive intelligence is the answer. And yes, it takes practice. Intuitive intelligence is remembering that we are a divine piece of a benevolent God that is always working on our behalf. To inhabit this mindset takes spiritual discipline and a willingness to trust the events of our life.

In 2014, I was doing the exact opposite. I had lost my faith in God. I was breaking the law, but it was easier to blame God, and that is what I did. Luckily for me, one single phone call brought me home.

The Second turning point

Archetype: Mother
Mantra: Thy will be done
Intuition Type: Creative intuition

2014. I was walking the dog by the creek near my house when my mother rang. I was walking mindlessly, a state I often inhabited at that time. I had been trying to hide from my myself, and I was worse for wear. Things were not going as I had planned. I had lost trust in the Infinite and so I was angry and on the run. As we know from the law of correspondence, what was really happening was that I did not trust *myself*, and the chaos that ensued was the Infinite coming into correspondence with my belief, so that I could overcome it. I had been raised knowing my spirituality as a part of my daily life since I was a tiny child.

In my mid- thirties I had experienced a profound crisis of faith. It was born of many things, including my belief that life – my life – would be simpler without it. I was on the run from my spiritual self, which of course meant I was on the run from myself. Until one call changed everything.

When the call from my mother came, I thought I was living the life I wanted. I had two beautiful children, a wonderful husband, and a career path I thought I wanted to pursue. It looked good on paper, and more importantly it was simple. Or so it seemed. Yet, I was an anxious mess, and in the end was diagnosed with a generalised anxiety disorder. I was prescribed Zoloft, which I took without question because I knew nothing could be worse than what I was feeling. I thought I had found the best way to live successfully but I was simply numbing my life. How had it reached this point? I had been a girl on fire – I knew everything I did, including my doctorate, was about bringing my vision of being a spiritual writer and teacher to life.

When I met my now husband several years earlier I was working in two ways, which reflects so much of my nature; as an intuitive reader in a crystal shop, running short courses on intuition activation, teaching a cohort of amazing women how to be professional intuitives, and I was completing my PhD at the University of Melbourne. My now husband was also completing his PhD and was already an accomplished and gainfully-employed academic. He was calm and kind and seemed to be much more in control of his life and emotions than I was at that time. I fell madly in love with him. I can see now how the seeds of my crisis of spiritual faith began with our union. Within a year or so of our relationship beginning I had stopped teaching intuition, and I had stopped working as a reader. I was offered a great role at the University that allowed me to pursue a path that was both exciting to me professionally and made my life easier. But there is so much more to understand about this time in my life than what first appears. This is not a case of a woman meeting a man and seeing all the answers to her life in him, although there is some of that. Certainly, part of me would have been very happy for a while to surrender my life to another at that point in my life.

However, the reality of my life was in fact very different to how I wanted it to be, especially in regard to the anger I felt within myself, and I was confused about it. Shouldn't the life of a spiritual seeker be happier than this?

I was very confused by my own emotional inconsistency, but I was as equally confused by my spiritual teacher's unhappy state. My mother, my first spiritual teacher, was also caught in an emotional storm much of the time. Very soon, I would understand the non-negotiable need to meet our fear above all else, and I would understand, too, the spiritual paradox with greater ease, but it was without doubt a turning point for me when I determined that I was more unhappy than happy most of the time. My beloved partner, a man of no mystical faith, seemed more content than I had ever been. I started to deeply question the things I had been raised to believe, and to turn away from my faith. Not because I didn't believe, but because my believing wasn't bringing me the rewards that, I guess, somewhere deep down I thought it would bring. These elements combined at a pivotal moment in my life, one in which I was offered an incredible job at the University of Melbourne. It seemed fated – the road diverged, and I took the path that seemed to add up. I really wanted to know if I could make it as an academic. My curious mind loves learning above all, and I wanted to be part of one of the greatest learning institutions in the world, but even that didn't go according to plan. The work wasn't satisfying me and seemed to be drying up before my eyes.

The (re)turning point came in the form of that unexpected and devastating phone call from my mother. It was June, mid-winter here in Australia, but the sun was blazing in the sky. My mum and I spoke almost every day. I can't remember now if she said it right away or if we talked for a time about other things, before she told me she had been to see her GP about her memory loss and low energy. He had informed her right there and then that she had Alzheimer's. Did I cry? I can't recall. What happened, though, was so swift and immediate that I will never forget. In a flash I could see my mother's life before my eyes – all the disappointments at not having shared her own incredible abilities as an intuitive, and her skills as a channel into the world. She wanted her spiritual work to be her life's work, and to be able to support herself with this. In her I could see my own life, the one I was hiding from.

I could see in an instant how she had never realised that dream, and in the same moment I knew I could be the one to make her dreams a reality. I did two things on the call that altered my life forever. I insisted she come to Melbourne for more testing – I was not going to accept that my mother's brilliant mind, and ultimately her life, could be ended in such an unforgiving way. And I made the offer that changed everything:

We'll go into business together. We'll call it Light-worker Institute.[18]

With that pronouncement the Infinite swept into action, and the dam I had been trying so desperately to hold back out of fear burst open. I was, finally, aligned with my joy. Within six months I was able to come off my anti-depressants, and I had more energy and joy coursing through me than I had had since I was a little girl. For as long as I could remember my dream was to be an international best-selling author of spiritual texts, and to travel the world sharing the wisdom of the Infinite to serve the awakening within me, within everyone.

But my commitment to this was hit-and-miss, and many times I readily took the path away from my soul's work. My dream life was a fully-realised spiritual path, but every time I came close to making that my full-time reality, I diverted off the path. Did I really want to meet my dream life? On the one hand I was saying *yes*, on the other my actions were saying "human chaos!". I hadn't yet awoken enough to reconcile those parts of myself, even though I thought I was fully aligned to the vision of my dream.

That phone call woke me up with an incredible jolt. It was as if everything became congruent between head and heart – or came into correspondence – and I set out on the road to the creation of the Institute with fearlessness and wonder. I had stepped into my spiritual maturity. I was willing to turn up with devotion and discipline to walk the path. I was finally making friends with my true nature and willingly, joyfully, surrendering the things that did not serve my higher purpose. I was on my path, and the inner and outer planes of my existence were in correspondence. I was willing to co-create my life in partnership with the Infinite and watch out! Because my creative energy was on fire and it hasn't slowed down since.

Know Thyself

Know thyself and thou shall know all the mysteries of the gods and of the universe.

Know thyself was inscribed above the entry at the Temple of Apollo at Delphi. It is an ancient and essential commandment for the spiritual seeker. The reason for its power is profoundly simple: when we investigate who and what we are beneath our fear, we meet the truth. Only love is real. Know thyself, and we meet ourselves in our pure state. All that exists is love. In that knowing we recognise that we are one with all that there is. Beyond the ego, beyond the identity, beyond our fear, is our unlimited self. Our ego keeps us working overtime in stories of unworthiness to prevent us from realising how unlimited we are, and how much power we possess. We must give up unworthiness now as an act of service to the planet. Playing small limits the possibility of our power to awaken to our true nature. We will know the mysteries of the gods and of the universe when we unlimit ourselves, because we will discover we are the God that we seek, and we are the whole Universe. *A Course in Miracles* states:

> *Whenever you question your value, say: God himself is incomplete without me.*

This is not ego, this is the opposite of ego. This is how we stay true to our path and do not allow ourselves to be induced by the temptation of the ego to be little and insignificant. The law of correspondence shows us that our work is to bring the inner world of our lives into correspondence with our true nature. This, of course, means knowing the contents of our subconscious mind. Our unmet fear resides here, and unless we go to meet it and clear it, the fear will rule our lives. In the following practice from Caroline Myss, we work archetypally to understand the nature of the fear that is predominant in our lives at any given time. Until we get to know what motivates us, we may not even understand how it has fear at its basis. *Know thyself* does not mean *ignore your fear*. In fact, the opposite is true. Like a warrior of love, you must meet your fear face-on so that it can be released, or transmuted into love.

The practice: the Intuitive Intelligence Micro Method (and a word on the nature of miracles)

The Intuitive Intelligence Method is a 75 minute one on one session with a qualified practitioner of the Method. These practitioners are trained by the Institute for Intuitive Intelligence. In a Method session, the client is guided to meet and clear the subconscious fear residing in her (or his) subtle anatomy and physical body. The practitioner acts as an intuitive guide to accelerate the process for the client.

The Intuitive Intelligence Micro Method is a simplified version of the full Method that allows whoever uses it to access the power of the Method for herself, and to have a robust tool to daily meet her fear. We must meet our fear every day to stay attuned to our intuitive intelligence, and when we apply the Micro Method to our fearful beliefs and physical symptoms we can quickly move the fear blocks out of our consciousness. It is these fear blocks that cause dis-ease in the body and mind. In vibration terms, the fear causes chaos at the level of the sub-atomic particle. When we change the vibration to a higher frequency we are simply restoring harmonic resonance at the sub-atomic level, and this is where all healing occurs.

In the Method, we open to the highest vibration feeling states and invite the Infinite to take that vibration to wherever it is needed most in ourselves. We ourselves are not diagnosing or determining where or how the Infinite should act to bring about a return to love in regard to this issue. We are letting that much more unlimited part of ourselves (remember, all is one) do the work, and we are simply the vessel. This is visionary intuition in action. We are not trying to heal or fix anything. We are moving beyond treating symptoms. We are opening to the possibility of the miracle – the immediate return to grace.

What is a miracle? When viewed through the laws, through which all things must be seen, it is overcoming the belief in separation, so that which is above is also below, what is within is also without, and that the vibration is of the feeling state of love. It is the transgression of the limits of belief of the receiver to return them to their right mind.

I want to take a moment to talk about the nature of miracles. *A Course in Miracles* tells us that we can only accept the miracle at the level our consciousness is able to receive it. This is directly related to how much fear a person carries in their consciousness. If we were to witness something that was beyond the scope of our capacity to believe – something beyond our limits – then it might strike fear into us, which is the opposite of the desired effect of the miracle. The miracle is an expression of an expansion in the limits of our belief. It makes sense that the more fear we release, the more we are able to receive miracles. We become, in fact, miracle-minded. When I speak of radical acceptance as the first step to things then actually changing positively around us, this is the science of which I speak. Expanding beyond our own current limits by meeting our fear permits the receipt of miracles. This from *A Course in Miracles*:

> *This means that a miracle, to attain its full efficacy, must be expressed in a language that the recipient can understand without fear. This does not necessarily mean that this is the highest level of communication of which he is capable. It does mean, however, that it is the highest level of communication of which he is capable now. The whole aim of the miracle is to raise the level of communication, not to lower it by increasing fear.*[19]

We are allowing the miracle to enter us, to transform us and to be released from our limits as a result. This is receptive power of the divine feminine in action. We simply cannot force a miracle into existence. It graces us and transforms us. Our job is to be open to receive it. We must be attuned to miracle-mindedness by removing the impediments to our true state, which is love. This is what the Method does, and I have seen it at work, producing miracles time and time again, releasing people in an instant from fear that took decades to acquire, or instantly removing trauma that appeared too far buried to ever remove.

The Method works with subconscious fear, for as *A Course in Miracles* tells us, we are never afraid for the reason we think we are. Our true fear sits beneath the surface of our conscious reasoning minds.

So, we apply the Micro Method to any stressful thought and in so doing release all the layers of the fear. The Micro Method moves us beyond self-awareness. We move directly from recognition of the fear into providing the exact conditions required to release that fear. This is a profoundly simple and elegant process. It can be practiced anywhere and at any time. The more often we do it, the more efficient we become at the process. We are building the muscle of our intuitive intelligence with spiritual fierceness by being willing to meet our fear every day. The Micro Method is an advanced practice of intuitive intelligence. It will work most powerfully for us when we have trained ourselves with practices such as Heart Congruence.

It is simple and direct but requires a commitment to live from the heart's intuitive intelligence. It is premised on the three immutable laws. The Infinite One Mind is waiting in every moment to guide us back to love. As such, the answers to show us *how* are always available when we create the optimal conditions for hearing that guidance. Practice the Micro Method with *blissipline* and be generously rewarded with the exact information required to be fearless. We are learning that we are able to consciously redirect our feeling states. This is particularly important when we remember that feeling is the language of the Infinite.

Here's how to use the Micro Method:

1. Notice the stressful thought or physical symptom
2. Close your eyes and take a deep breath in through your nose, letting it go out through your mouth with an audible sigh. Maintain a slightly extended breath, breathing in for four counts and out for 6 counts
3. Rate the stressful thought or physical symptom on a scale of 1-10, 10 being the most intense. Our aim is to bring that number down with the Micro Method
4. Place two fingers at the centre of your chest
5. Ask slightly or out loud, *what is the dominant fear in this situation?*
   a. The answer will be brief and succinct and will make itself known to you through your dominant clair (clairsentience, clairaudience, claircognisance or clairvoyance). You will see, hear, feel or know the answer. It will be as brief as one word, image, sound or short phrase. Intuition is instant and precise.
6. Now, turn your attention to mental images and thoughts that invoke feelings of deep gratitude. It may be the smile of your child, the sun on your back, the memory of a holiday. It must bring up for you only the high vibrational feeling of gratitude. You must give yourself over to this feeling with your whole being. Let it build for around one minute. Allow the feeling to expand in you with as much intensity as possible. Now let go of the feelings of gratitude
7. Take a deep breath in and let it go out through the mouth

8. Look around for the stressful thought or physical symptom that you rated on a scale of 1-10. When you find it, rate it again. If the number is above 2, repeat Step (6) up to two more times.

Meeting the Infinite within

The very morning, I sat to write this chapter, the idea for which had been circulating in my mind and heart for several days, I had a big *To Do list*. I woke up knowing that I needed to meditate. I meditate every day, but this morning it was a stronger call, yet I resisted it. I picked up my iPhone, checked my social media accounts, and then jumped in the shower. I told myself I would meditate in the shower. It was the first day back at work for me in the New Year, 2016, and I was keen to get through a long list of mundane chores, so I could focus on writing this book. I had to get my toddler to daycare, and as I stepped out of the shower, without having meditated, my thoughts were already turning to that transition out of the house and into the car, and the enormous amounts of patience and perseverance it takes to negotiate a 3-year-old into his car seat. He wanted to play a game with me on the iPad as I was pushing his little running shoes onto his feet. I sat with him as he showed me how to steer a car all over the screen, and even then, the overwhelming pull to sit in meditation called me. I tried to surreptitiously assume the position on the bed next to the toddler as he smashed cars into one another with glee, but he wasn't having it. He knew he didn't have my full attention, and I knew I was getting nowhere with this meditation.

Instead, I decided just to bundle him into the car and get on with the day and the busy list. There would be time to meditate later. As we arrived at daycare and I dispatched my little one into the arms of his carers, and I hopped back into the car ready to pounce on the list, the call to meditate was only growing in intensity. My ego mind tried desperately to negotiate with me and negate this powerful energy:

Just do half the list, then go home and meditate!
You cannot go home without achieving something on that list!
You will be letting people down! You have a plan. Stick to the plan!

But my soul voice was louder. The ego became more desperate as I became more serene. I turned the car into my street and headed home. A wave of peace washed over me. Finally, I was listening. What bliss to surrender to my intuitive knowing. The desire to be in meditation now was so absolute that I would have walked across hot coals to get to my sacred space. I almost ran inside, and lit incense and candle and assumed my half-lotus position on my meditation cushion. Saraswati, the Hindu Goddess of the arts, knowledge, music, and learning, looked upon me from her pride of place on the altar. I have loved her since the moment I learnt about her some two years earlier. I understood her deep longing to be left alone to the inner workings of the mind and the soul, to be in contemplation and reflection. For two days now, I had heard the call of Saraswati within me to sit in stillness and write, but life had not allowed it. Now it did, and she was not taking no for an answer.

I could feel the power build as I sat. One breath, two, three, and I was already deeply immersed in the energy of deep meditation. This is of course what happens with a systematic mediation practice, but today held extra power and it was effortless to assume this state of profound peace. I could hear the monkey mind chattering away, but it was as though it was in another room, not front and centre as it often feels to be, and it was easy to ignore. It felt as if it was someone else's mind I was overhearing and, as such, I had no attachment to what was being thought. Instantly I felt the heart activation begin. Ah, yes! Now, I understood the urgency of this call to be in meditation. For several days now, since the beginning of the New Year, I had felt my heart energy intensely. Why was this happening? I had an idea. It had been my cry for my entire adult life to release me from the grip of the lower emotions, especially anger, and to surrender to my open heart. For so long it had felt like I had been doing this work in the dark – on blind faith in other words – without seeing the result I sought, which was to know peace. Not fleetingly, but all the time. As the New Year dawned on 2016 I set only one simple intention:

Lord, make me an instrument of your peace.

This is the first line of the prayer of St Francis, and it had been swirling around my mind for weeks.

As the days of 2016 unfolded I could feel this call to be at peace changing and evolving my consciousness. I could feel it especially when I did yoga. On those occasions I saw the heart chakra at the centre of my chest being activated in my mind's eye. That day in meditation, the next vital step in this activation took place. No wonder I needed to be in this state of silence, rather than running around like a headless chicken! What a terrible loss it would have been to lay waste to my day in such an unnecessary way, rather than surrendering to the very thing I have been so long desiring and calling for. The Infinite was literally trying to answer my prayers, and all I had to do was surrender my very mundane plans. And yet, even with such an ordinary day ahead of me, the ego still resisted the change. In truth, the ego, a divine and blessed part of me, knew what was coming and of course would resist my soul's evolution at any cost. It simply could not permit my evolution, because it knew it means its death. If it died and I was it, according to the ego, then it was doing its utmost to save my life! Even the sabotaging efforts of the ego mind could be seen as great love from the right perspective! As the meditation went on, I felt the energy move to my third eye. I felt like the statue of Saraswati on my altar had come to life and was standing in front of me. I knew it was the energy of this Goddess guiding me. I had been reading about her the night before and I knew, from my place of intuitive knowing, that she was now gifting me with a direct experience of her love and power, and most importantly her unique gift of clear creative expression, something I desired so much at the time.

All my life I have been a writer in one way or another, first as a playwright, and then as an academic. All I have ever wanted to do is write a spiritual text. The attempts have been innumerable and yet always I stopped – I gave up before the finish line. I was suddenly aware that this process that was now going on within me that was lovingly and gently clearing me of this block. Saraswati was an enormous and generous piece of this puzzle. She was gifting me with the knowledge of divine timing and permission to seek the time to focus on my creativity without apology. To be who I knew myself to be. As the meditation continued I felt myself tuned into a vibrational frequency far higher and lighter than I had felt before. What a divine gift! What would I have missed if I had ignored the intuitive call! In my mind I could see a beam of light literally like a unicorn's horn, tuning me into this high vibrational frequency, then I watched as this moved from my crown chakra to my third eye, then to all the other chakra points on my body, and then beams of light sprung forth on the front and back of my body. I was connected in a way I have never been before. I was tuned into the most perfect frequency for me to complete this text and to walk the path I have seen for myself for decades. I felt clear. As the energy began to abate I moved to my desk and began to write. This book is the result of that experience.

Intuitive intelligence is everything we have just read. It is answering the call to come home when I had made other plans; it is the divine blessing I received when I surrendered and meditated instead of rushing about. It is knowing that when I closed my eyes in meditation, and the stunning green mandala that is the heart grid appeared before me, that I was being lovingly activated in this moment. How easy it would be to dismiss this as the mind or imagination running away with me. And yet when I reflected, I remember that I had in fact dedicated that year to the activation of peace within me. It is knowing that I am worthy of being one that the Goddess speaks to, for I am she and she is me, and that my call the previous night to read a chapter in a book about Saraswati, even though it meant reading the book out of order, was not a casual accident.

Her consciousness was seeding mine even then (and for years before that, too). It was an intentional design to allow me to know, to profoundly intuit, her energy when she came to me in meditation that very morning. I could recognise her without doubt and receive her blessings openly. It is knowing that when I see a beam of light emerging from the top of my head and connecting me to the outer limits of cosmic consciousness, I am not being messed with. It is trusting that the Infinite is simply finding joyful and imaginative ways to communicate very big ideas to me, and that this visualising capacity that I have is one of the most profound intuitive capacities I (and we all) possess. It is knowing when the time is right to leap joyfully from the meditation cushion to the desk to begin to transcribe one of the most important moments of my soul's evolution. The moment I was invited into my sacred heart.

For all of us – and for me that day – it became so clear that intuitive intelligence is not dismissing all of this as a joke of the mind, or worse, an experience that we simply are not worthy of. For we know that as a piece of the Infinite, we don't have time for low self-worth. Intuitive intelligence is knowing our worth because we are a voice of divine perfection. It is trusting the vision of our life that we were given in meditation, trusting in divine timing, and trusting the Infinite, and trusting that every time we trust we deepen that connection and bond, and that it can and will grow as a result. The more we listen to our intuition, the more we hear our intuition. The more we surrender, even when it is inconvenient in daily life, the more quickly we come into alignment with our soul's destiny. The more we give in to our intuitive knowing, the more quickly the Infinite rushes to bring the people, places, events, and tools we require together that make reality the vision of our life.

This is surrender in action. This is living with intuitive intelligence.

The role of our nonlocal guides

Intuition as we know by now is the language of the soul. It is how God communicates with us. We are connected directly to God without mediation. Intuition is the hotline. God is Infinite and, as we now understand from the law of correspondence, will show up for us in accordance with our belief. Guides, angels, nature spirits, animal guides, the Goddess in all her forms (as we have witnessed in the previous chapter), God, loved ones who have crossed over – all the invisible, nonlocal support team – are there if we choose to connect to them. We connect to them as part of *what we are*. You might notice in that list that I don't privilege any one being of light over another. Recently-deceased people sit right alongside God. There is a reason for this. In truth, all is one. The faces, personalities, identities and feelings we associate with any given member of the invisible support team is as much for our benefit as it is akin to their true nature. Just as we take on a form to manifest in the world, so it is with our nonlocal support team. The Infinite takes on a form, a personality, so we may have a more immediate relationship with it.

Look at it this way: the law that *all is one* is as true on the earthly plane as it is in the invisible realms. Yet most of us do not walk around identifying everyone we see as an innate aspect of ourselves. We are seven billion faces of one energy. Our invisible support team is an individuated expression of one divine essential energy or truth. The Infinite is within. This is the starting point for communication with all the faces of the Infinite. You are not reaching out into the Infinite. You are reaching in, *into* the Infinite. As above, so below. As within, so without. The outer world is a mirror of our inner world. When we go to meet the ascended masters or animal spirit, we go to the Infinite within. God is everything. For example, we are meeting a face of God when we connect to a specific ascended master. But within the part is the whole.

Byron Katie tells this story of communicating with her "guide" at a particularly difficult time in her life after she woke up to her Infinite nature:

What I have come to know is that I projected the lady ... like a movie ... as a result of painful limitations I was experiencing in this dimension. We give ourselves exactly what we need. We supply our own medicine ... Today I don't wait for angels. I am always the angel I have been awaiting, and so are you. It's not out there, it's in here ... some people would project Christ, others Krishna ... I projected a fat lady with a bun on her head wearing a paisley dress – that's who I could trust. Now I trust all. I woke up knowing that God is everything ... there is no exception in my experience.[20]

This story explains what it is to connect to our guides in whatever form they take. If we privilege the personality of the guide, then we believe in separation. If we respond to our guides archetypally, their meaning and role in our life is suddenly very clear. Why would I be so drawn to Jesus, the greatest healer the world has ever known? The qualities embodied by the Christ Consciousness are qualities I aspire to embody. The archetype is the framework around which I can build my own consciousness. Is Jesus any less real to me because I am conjuring him from within? No, he is more real, for I have overcome my faulty belief in separation. Communication with our nonlocal guides in this way can be thought of as a form of consciousness engineering. We are up-levelling our consciousness by holding the consciousness of what we can become within our hearts and minds. We are showing our consciousness how we want it to behave. This is very liberating.

For example, we may tune into our intuitive intelligence one day and we find that wolf consciousness is very close to us, and that it feels like a wolf has sat at our feet. It has come to us for a reason. Trusting that its energy has a gift for us at this moment in our life is intuition in action. As we grow our intuitive intelligence, this kind of experience becomes commonplace. But it will most likely always be subtle and, therefore, easily missed if life is busy. If we do notice this wolf energy following us around, for example, then this is an excellent time to sit down in meditation, tune in, and invite this energy to let us know what it has for us. It may well be that we have a mighty transition coming up in our life (a new job, home, relationship, or an ending of any or all of these), and the mystical strength of the wolf energy is here to guard our space and show us the deeper meaning of the unfolding of these events. Once we have connected to this energy it becomes a power source for us, a totem, and an active reminder that we are not limited to local support alone.

Trusting these events is a sign of a strengthening intuition, and the more we take time to notice these events the more frequently they occur. In fact, we are then able to invite the Infinite to work through us in deliberate ways and times. For example, we might have been learning about angels and we are very keen to directly commune with an angel. If we take the time to prepare the space and conditions for this to happen, then the angelic realm will respond. More often than not, the fact that we have angels on our radar all of a sudden is a sign that the angels have been preparing for us, and not the other way around! In other words, if we feel drawn to communicate with a particular face of the Infinite, the seeds of that idea have probably been sown by that unlimited consciousness, as was my experience with Saraswati. As above, so below. I had a client session recently and as I sat to prepare, a book all about the ascended masters kept grabbing my attention. It was on the bookcase next to me, but it felt like it was jumping off the shelf trying to get into my hands. Eventually I gave in and recognised that in this session we were going to take the client to meet her guide. Without question this book was letting me know that the client's personal guide was one of the Brotherhood of Light[21].

In this instance, I was told which of the masters was guiding her, although this doesn't always happen. It was very clear that this guide wanted to be connected to my client without any doubt in either of our minds. Connecting to the right member of our invisible support team at the right time can profoundly deepen our sense of connection to our intuition and deepen our knowing that we are not alone in this journey, one that often feels like a journey of blind faith. Simply know that, like us, these beings are messengers of divine consciousness, and that ultimately one energy unites us all.

The individual faces of the Infinite that we commune with will change frequently. Our personal guide may stay with us for years, but from day to day we will discover that where we are in the world, the work we are doing, the project we are trying to bring into being – all the variables of our life – will determine who or what comes to our aid. If we are hiking in nature, for example, we attune far more easily to the devas, nature spirits, and elementals than if we are in a high-rise office block. We also notice that we attune to one kind of invisible support team far more than others (also, this will also most likely change over the course of your life). I work with the Brotherhood of Light most strongly. I have a client who is deeply connected to animals, and in both the astral and physical planes animals follow her. She cannot go anywhere without being met by a murder of crows. These birds are her totem, and as she makes big changes in her life she is continually reminded of the support from the invisible realms by their presence. Don't mistake me here: these crows are living, breathing birds, not spirit animals, although I am sure she has those, too. Animals are by nature multidimensional, and by that, I mean they communicate easily with the Infinite and act directly as messengers because of their egoless state.

A note on angels and guides

As I understand it, we are all born with a Guardian Angel, and this being of light stays with us for the duration of our earthly life. I have not directly communicated with my Guardian Angel often. When the communication does happen, it is wordless love flowing into my being. My Guardian Angel stands or floats behind me always and wraps his or her wings around me (angels are gender-neutral, although our mind's eye will generally show them to us as male or female). We are also assigned a personal guide, and this guide will change throughout our lives based on the place we are at and the specific support we need. This guide will communicate with you at will and easily because that is their very role. Our guides will usually show themselves to us in the guise of a previous lifetime in which they have walked the earth. They often take on human form to connect with us to give us the ease of familiarity, although it is not uncommon for the students I have worked with to simply feel a quality rather than have an image of their guide in their mind's eye. All of this is absolutely perfect. Our guides are as unique as we are. There are Infinite numbers of beings willing and joyously awaiting to work with us. I am keeping this section brief intentionally. There are many resources out there already about the myriad of our invisible support team. Doreen Virtue has a great number of books and resources on the topic. All consciousness is communicating. We can tap into this at any time, although it won't always be to get information. Rather, this communion with the invisible consciousness is a direct reminder of the unifying energy that moves through all of us, that *is* us. If it works better for you, go straight to God. Our guides are simply showing up in accordance with our belief about them.

I am much more interested in our connection to the unlimited consciousness that pervades everything, that is us. Individuating divine consciousness into the different kinds of divine support team is exciting and allows us to form intimate connection to this energy. If we are moving towards healing our minds of the wounded belief in separateness, then ultimately, I want us to remember: that which we are communicating with is us. It is vibrating at a higher frequency than us simply because it doesn't have to hold form together in the way that we do. Unfettered by the problems of locality and limited consciousness, our invisible support team is freewheeling, tuned-in and so much clearer on the truth of our nature. And what is the truth of our nature? Well, that's the story of this entire book. Love. Love is all there is. If all there is, is Love, and you are all that is, then without question you must be love. It's science.

The practice: meet your guide

Knowing that the Infinite and all possible guides are within, it helps us to understand better how we might access these individuated pieces of the Infinite. It is very joyful to go on a journey to meet members of our current support, remembering these archetypal energies show up as the medicine we need at any given time and may change. This journey can be taken as often as you like and will deepen your sense of intimacy and connectedness to the divine.

- Sit somewhere with your spine straight ensuring you won't be disturbed.
- Close your eyes and deepen your breath, signifying to your physiology that you are very safe.
- Notice in your mind's eye a doorway. Notice its size, shape and colour. Walk over to the door, signalling your intention to go deeper. The door opens effortlessly in front of you and you walk through it. You find yourself in a vast field of white flowers. Notice the time of day, the temperature. Feel the gentle breeze on your skin and your favourite scent in the air. The sunlight or moonlight reflects off the flowers, illuminating everything around you. You feel very relaxed and ready.
- You notice a small green hill in front of you with a winding path leading up the gentle slope to the top. You begin to make your way, one step at a time, effortlessly walking up higher, and higher, and higher. You reach the top of the hill and you notice a grove of trees in front of you. You can hear running water and you make your way towards it, entering the grove of trees. It is cool and calm here, and you walk towards the babbling brook and gaze into the clear blue water. Beside the brook is a large flat stone, perfect for sitting upon. You climb onto the ancient stone and you sit. You lean forward and cup your fingers into the icy blue water and sip. As you look up, you notice with curiosity that there is someone seated opposite you on an identical stone, smiling at you, and the guide feels very familiar, very loving.
- This is your personal guide. Take some time to observe the guide. They do not mind this attention. Notice their hair colour, their gender, what they are wearing. You may have met them before, or not, it doesn't matter. You fix your gaze upon them now, and they continue to smile lovingly.

- You now ask them their name, which they will happily share with you. Be open to how you receive this information. It may like a voice stating the name, or a flash of colour, or an image or a feeling. Allow the name to come in whatever way it will, or not at all if that is what happens. Resist jumping into your mind here. You might want this guide to be someone in particular, and if that is the case you aren't judgment free and you'll block your intuitive knowing. The name will come when it is ready. For example, you might see the same name everywhere you go in the coming days. This is the Infinite communicating with you. Don't dismiss this miracle as chance or coincidence.

- Ask now if your guide has anything they would like to share with you. Allow anything that happens to happen, knowing that you are very safe, and this guide is a face of the Infinite one mind, which is pure love. You may notice your guide stands and beckons you to them to embrace you. They may wordlessly send you love. They may have a message of one word or a hundred! Stay in this space with your guide for as long as you feel to do so, and allow the meeting to transpire, as it will.

- When you feel your time is complete, you stand and thank your guide. You bow to them and them to you, honouring the reverence of this meeting. You step down off the rock and turn, noticing a doorway before you. You walk towards the door and it opens effortlessly before you. You walk through it easily, and you find yourself in your room, on your chair. Take a deep breath. Open your eyes.

You can revisit this place as often as you like. Your guide will always be there to meet you. Or you may notice that the more you practice connecting to your invisible support team the less you need to "go" anywhere to communicate with them. This is a powerful meditation to step out of ordinary reality for a time, however, and it is incredibly renewing. As the optimal conditions in which intuitive intelligence flourish are stillness, silence, and solitude, it makes sense to make the journey to this sacred hilltop as a way of deepening your connection to your own Infinite nature.

Getting in the Gap

There is one essential quality we need to bring into our life to be intuitively intelligent. Remember, intuition is just a symptom. It is a symptom of remembering how connected and supported we are to and by the Infinite. We have to remind ourselves of this connected state every day, because the world of local human reality and everything in it is actively working to make us forget. This isn't a conspiracy, but simply an indicator of sickness. The sickness is that of forgetting. Our whole Western world is suffering from a terrible amnesia that is perpetuated by our belief in our separateness. We have forgotten our true nature, and so we create mirages around us that confirm that forgetting in this worldview. We are then not divine aspects of a harmonious oneness. We are small, separate, isolated, lonely consumers, desperately trying to fill up the void with useless stuff that ultimately is impermanent, fragile, and loses its value quickly. That's how we think about ourselves. That's where the problems start and end.

As the law of correspondence shows us reality, whatever we are living now is simply a reflection of our unhealed minds. Intuitive intelligence is a symptom of healed mind.

Reality as a reflection of our belief system doesn't just happen at the individual level. In fact it never does.

We attract people and experiences to us that mirror our beliefs about the world. That's the very essence of the why of activating our intuition. We want to change our set point, or the level of belief we are carrying at any given time, to allow us to receive more and more of the good stuff.

The more we live from our intuition, the more we come into congruence with our unlimited nature. Why? Because intuition is direct instruction from the Infinite, and the Infinite always has our back. God is our partner, our partner who is divinely, blissfully, and unconditionally in love with us. It is guiding us towards our best life in every moment. The sickness in our minds is what prevents us from receiving that guidance, and the unworthiness in our hearts is what stops us from listening to it even when we hear it. Whoa! Sick and unworthy? How on earth do we overcome this set of obstacles to receive the loving guidance from our all-knowing, brilliant partner? I'm not going to sugar-coat this: we have to take our medicine. And yes, there is a medicine to overcome the sick mind and the wounded heart. In fact, there are many medicines, and this book has a whole bunch of them. This is yet another one, and without question the most vital, because it is the foundation of all the others. It isn't easy but with spiritual fierceness it is also not hard, and in time it will become effortless and joyful and non-negotiable.

Meditation.

Following is a technique that is not only going to make meditation possible for you, but also impossible to fail at. I get quite excited when people tell me that they can't meditate. I start waving my hands in the air and muttering about speaking French and not quitting after one failed attempt to order *café au lait* and *croissant* at the local patisserie. What I mean to say is this: we can meditate. Oh yes, we can *all* meditate.

Let's begin with why we would want to, because in regard to being the unlimited consciousness we already are, the act of meditation might begin to make perfect sense. Why is meditation such a big deal to the intuitive? There is a spiritual idea called *getting in the gap*. Quite simply, this means finding space between the thoughts of the monkey-mind. This is done to reach the state of peace that allows ourselves to know our true nature, our sacred nature. In the gap between thoughts, between emotions, there resides Infinite Consciousness. The work of our lives as intuitives is to spend as much time as possible in that gap, the space of the eternal. But we cannot think ourselves there. We cannot force ourselves there. We can only reach this space by surrender. What does that mean? It means we make time and space for the gap, even when we do not know if we will reach it that day, or that month, or that year. We make the time regardless because, ultimately, we know it is the only way to meet our co-creative partner. It is the only way to access our divine natures and live the fullness of our lives.

Meditation is all about getting in the space between our illusory beliefs about the nature of ourselves and the world we inhabit, in order to allow the truth of ourselves to become more and more present. It is a process, and there are steps. This is, as I have said, the foundation of all the other practices I share with you in this book. This is also the foundation of all other practices. Meditation has scientific and strong physiological evidence backing up its benefits. I always meditate with the sacred in mind, but I also know that with raging anxiety or manic stress I am not going anywhere, let alone into the Infinite. It helps to think of the practical aspects of meditating as a way to motivate our practice, especially when we begin.

Here are some great reasons why meditation should be a non-negotiable health and well-being practice: more than 150 studies have demonstrated the positive impacts of mediation on reducing anxiety. Some 90% of people with anxiety who undertook a meditation practice experienced a significant reduction in anxiety.[22] Meditation supports the part of the brain that manages stress, so that we are less stressed when we meditate. Stress is neurotoxic to the brain and prevents us from being in a heart-coherent state. Whilst Heart Congruence and meditation are different practices, we usually can't get into a meditative state without Heart Congruence. I recommend beginning with the technique introduced in Chapter Two as a prelude to meditation. It will rapidly increase the ease of the meditation experience, and if it is easeful you are likely to want to do it again. Eventually, meditation will become a total non-negotiable because it feels so good.

The practice: increase the gap between your heartbeats

The purpose of this technique is to take us to the space between, to the gap, the home of our intuition.

- Be seated, your spine straight but soft – there is nothing rigid about the body in meditation, for stillness is the aim. If the body is held too tightly there will be no stillness. If you are tired, overwhelmed, resistant, or reticent then please lie down. Remember, it is a step-by-step process, so if step one for you is to be lying down, then do it! There is no impediment to your meditation practice too big to overcome. Don't *not* meditate because of some mental image of what meditation looks like that you don't believe you are meeting.

- Take your pulse by counting the beats at the radial artery for fifteen seconds.
- Write it down.
- Then set your timer on your phone for five minutes. Make sure your phone is in flight mode.
- Focus on your breath. Deepen your breathing, extending the length of each in breath and out breath. Add a pause between the inhalation and exhalation.
- Continue for five minutes.
- Take your pulse again. The aim is for less beats in that first fifteen-second measure.

Okay, we have just changed our lives for good. What's that? This little technique has profoundly increased our Heart Rate Variability (HRV) – that is, the space between our heartbeats. One of the most powerful tools for change we have is to spend as much time as we can in the gap between our heartbeats. This is the sacred space in which we are in communion with the Infinite. Nearly twenty-five years of clinical research has shown that, when HRV levels are high, people can experience lower stress levels and greater resilience.[23]

If we want to be in communion with the highest part of ourselves and engineer the Universe in accordance with our highest good, then we need to increase our HRV, reduce our heart rate, and get in the gap. There are stories of great mystics and yogis who can lower their heart rate to such an extent that they appear as though they are dead. This is not a party trick. The intention is to be in a state of mastery of our physiological responses. When we can alter our own heart rate, we are able to prevent the lower emotional states from controlling us. We can literally breathe our way back into harmony.

The temporal location of intuitive Intelligence

Find the 'narrow gate that leads to life'. It is called the Now. Narrow your life down to this moment. Your life situation may be full of problems – most life situations are – but find out if you have any problem at this moment. Not tomorrow or in ten minutes, but now. Do you have a problem now?

— Eckhart Tolle

I stood in the shower, the water running over me on full blast, hot and steamy. I could hardly feel it though. I was lost in thought. My mind was in a panic, but I could not locate the reason why. All I knew was that anxiety was rushing through me, wave after wave, and I was barely conscious of the moment I was in. Who knows how long I stood there in the shower? I was lost in my mind. I was lost in thoughts about the past or the future, I couldn't tell which, but I knew that somewhere along the line I had attached myself to a particular thought that was now robbing me of the bliss of the present moment. I leaned my head against the tiled shower recess and tried to get the mess in my mind into some kind of order. What had sparked this sudden riot of fear and stress in my body?

Suddenly, I found the stress-inducing thought. I had booked a weekend workshop and paid a hefty deposit for the venue. I was so excited about the availability of the space that I hadn't double-checked the date. That morning my best friend reminded me that it was a long weekend. My heart sank. Why hadn't I double-checked? I was certain it would be a complete disaster and I would be lumped with an expensive, empty venue! I tried to laugh it off in the moment, but a sense of dread kept building up in me throughout the day. By the time I stood in the shower I was an anxious mess. My fear of future failure was so complete that I couldn't see around it. My ego was telling me one thing: *you're doomed!* I went into action, of course, applying all the techniques that I share in this book, but before I tell you more about what I did to recover myself from the grip of my ego fear, let's look at what was happening, and how easy it is to confuse intuition with fear when we don't heed the temporality of the information we are getting.

The very moment I found the venue for my training and booked it, my energy had been high and light. It felt amazing. The date felt right. The space felt right. I was uplifted and joyful as I paid the deposit. Bookings for the workshop were rolling in. I was in the present moment, trusting my feeling state as it fed me intuitive signals in the form of lightness and joy in my body.

Then, the very moment I found out that it was a long weekend (ergo, no one would come!) my fear kicked in. The ego mind took over and started to tell me stories of disaster of an unknown and unknowable future. I was so far out in that fearful future story that I completely checked out from my own body. As I stood in the shower, I lost all sense of time and sensation. The water was falling but I was not feeling it. I was lost in an imaginary future. I was in the prison of my mind, and that prison was in the future. The point is this: anytime I leave the present moment, I am disconnected from my intuition.

Intuition lives in the present. Intuition is now. All that ever was and ever will be is now. The past and the future do not exist in fixed locations separate from this time and space. They exist now. There is only now. As Gregg Braden states: "The matrix [the Infinite] appears to be the container that holds time, providing for continuity between the experiences of our present and those of the future". When we go into obsessive thoughts about the past or the future and lose ourselves in the stress and anxiety of those imaginary places, we lose ourselves. We lose our connection to the Infinite wisdom of God. We have fallen into a nightmare of our own making, and we must be roused to bring ourselves back to this moment now. In that moment, in the shower, as I awoke to the nightmare, I used Emotional Freedom Technique (EFT – more on this in a moment) to guide myself out of the maze of panic and anxiety. I had tapped into the fear of failure; a fear that was born out observing the past and making a story out of it and lived in the future holding my happiness to ransom. Of course, it all existed inside of me in this moment, but my ego had created a temporal narrative out of events. The small thing of choosing a long weekend to run a workshop had turned in a catastrophic failure based on an immutable history and an unkind future. It was nothing turned into everything.

It was also a gift, because it showed me the subconscious fears inside of myself that needed more work. The fear always shows up as a gift to be released. It showed me where I was being dragged away from my own happiness, where I was being removed from my intuition.

The workshops were perfect, with the perfect number and combination of people there. My intuition in choosing the time and place was spot on. The workshops were, of course, never the cause of the stress and anxiety. They simply provided the opportunity for me to uncover ego fear and to bring myself back to the moment. The fear voice, the voice of the ego when it has forgotten its place in service to the whole and has tried once more to be master, was trying its very best to convince me that I had made a mistake. It was trying to pass itself off as my intuition. Eventually I could recognise this by two things:

- Intuition is immediate and instant. In making the booking I was being guided. In the moment I knew my truth. It was only when the ego fear had time to seduce me in my vulnerability that I started to question myself.
- Intuition comes with peace. Another way to think about this is intuition comes with a feeling of certainty. Even when our intuition is guiding us towards something difficult – and perhaps not something we want – we will know its truth by a pervading sense of calm, in the moment. In the moment of our decision or action we will feel certainty.

Fear doesn't live in the present. In the present moment, in the now, all is as it should be. It always is. It cannot be any other way. This is a big concept to get our heads around, but it is the essence of understanding the difference between intuition and ego fear. In this moment now, we can trust the information we are receiving from the Infinite. When we feel an impulse to turn left instead of right and we trust it and follow that impulse, even though our mind may be telling us that we always go right, and we should do that now, we are in the moment and we are listening to your intuition. If we hesitate, and turn right because that is what we have always done, and that in the past turning left has led to all kinds of trouble, then we have abandoned the present, intuition-full moment, and gone back into the past. We are listening to an old story about how left always leads to trouble and has never worked out for us.

There is an important distinction to be made here. Wisdom that comes from having lived and learnt is not to be ignored. There have probably been a hundred times when we have simply gone right because we know from experience it is the best path. But in that moment of feeling inspired to go left, to ignore the intuitive impulse is to ignore the God voice. Every time we trust our intuition, even if we do not know why, we strengthen our connection to our intuition. We open to it even more consciously and wed ourselves even more powerfully to the present. Intuition is instant. We may not receive the answer to our question immediately, but when the answer comes we will know it is our intuition speaking in the way that it instantly occupies us with certainty and a sense of heightened energy. The mind may step in quickly to make us doubt that intuitive knowing, but it will not succeed when we have done the work of clearing our blocks.

The practice: EFT

Gary Craig originally created Emotional Freedom Technique or tapping. EFT is a psychological acupressure technique I use in my practice, and with my clients and students. It is simply the most powerful, totally free and readily-available tool we have on the planet to remove from within us the subconscious blocks to love. Its efficacy and usability make it second-to- none in regard to the tools we need to use to combat our fear. There is nothing that is outside of tapping's capacity. The beauty of this resource is that it allows us to peel back the layers of our fearful thinking, to access the subconscious level of our fear, and release it quickly and permanently.

Tapping uses the body's meridian points in the same way acupuncture does. Everything is energy, and fear is a disruption to the healthy flow of that energy in our bodies and our consciousness. Tapping repairs the healthy flow of energy – which we can also think of as prana, chi, or grace by working energetically through the meridian lines in the body.

I encourage my clients to work intuitively rather than follow scripts. When we have created the right conditions for intuitive intelligence to flourish we are more readily able to start a dialogue with our subconscious mind, and to speak the fears that are controlling us. Just speak in a stream of consciousness as we tap through the points and allow the dark to be brought into the light. It can be confronting to speak our fears out loud because we mostly avoid our fear, and that of course is the problem.

We are literally drawing out the toxic fear when we tap and returning to our true state, which is love. It's my very strong belief that we don't need to tap on the "positive" because when we remove the fear, we *are* the positive! Our natural state is love. Fear is not real. It is an illusion. We simply need to clear it and be returned to our state of love.

I am sharing with you the "how to" of tapping taken from Nick Ortner'[24] who has been part of bringing EFT into the mainstream. So how to tap? From Nick's *The Tapping Solution*, this example focuses on the feeling of anxiety.

Try it now with this initial sequence. Here's how a basic tapping sequence works:

- Identify the problem you want to focus on. It can be general anxiety, or it can be a specific situation or issue, which causes you to feel anxious.

- Consider the problem or situation. How do you feel about it right now? Rate the intensity level of your anxiety, with zero being the lowest level of anxiety and ten being the highest.
- Compose your set-up statement. Your set-up statement should acknowledge the problem you want to deal with, then follow it with an unconditional affirmation of yourself as a person. These could include affirmations such as

> *Even though I feel this anxiety, I deeply and completely accept myself.*
> *Even though I'm anxious about my interview, I deeply and completely accept myself.*
> *Even though I'm feeling this anxiety about my financial situation, I deeply and completely accept myself.*
> *Even though I panic when I think about, I deeply and completely accept myself.*
> *Even though I'm worried about how to approach my boss, I deeply and completely accept myself.*
> *Even though I'm having trouble breathing, I deeply and completely accept myself.*

- Perform the set-up. With four fingers on one hand, tap the karate chop point on your other hand – the karate chop point is on the outer edge of the hand, on the opposite side from the thumb. Repeat the set-up statement three times aloud, while simultaneously tapping the karate chop point.
- Now take a deep breath! Get ready to begin tapping!

Here are some tips to help you achieve the right technique:

- You should use a firm but gentle pressure, as if you were drumming on the side of your desk or testing a melon for ripeness.
- You can use all four fingers, or just the first two (the index and middle finger). Four fingers are generally used on the top of the head, the collarbone, under the arm ... wider areas. On sensitive areas, such as around the eyes, you can use just two.
- Tap with your fingertips, not your fingernails. The sound will be round and mellow.
- The tapping order begins at the top and works down. You can end by returning to the top of the head, to complete the loop.

Now, tap 5–7 times each on the remaining eight points in the following sequence:

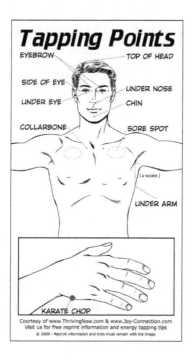

Head (TH) — The crown, centre and top of the head. Tap with all four fingers on both hands.

Eyebrow (EB) — The inner edges of the eyebrows, closest to the bridge of the nose. Use two fingers.

Side of eye (SE) — The hard area between the eye and the temple. Use two fingers. Feel out this area gently so you don't poke yourself in the eye!

Under eye (UE) — The hard area under the eye, that merges with the cheekbone. Use two fingers, in line beneath the pupil.

Under nose (UN) — The point centred between the bottom of the nose and the upper lip. Use two fingers.

Chin (CP) — This point is right beneath the previous one, and is centred between the bottom of the lower lip and the chin.

Collarbone (CB) — Tap just below the hard ridge of your collarbone with four fingers.

Underarm (UA) — On your side, about four inches beneath the armpit. Use four fingers.

Head (TH) — And back where you started, to complete the sequence.

As you tap on each point, repeat a simple reminder phrase, such as "my anxiety", or "my interview", or "my financial situation".

Now take another deep breath!

- Now that you've completed the sequence, focus on your problem again. How intense is the anxiety now, in comparison to a few minutes ago? Give it a rating on the same number scale.

- If your anxiety is still higher than 2/10, you can do another round of tapping. Keep tapping until the anxiety is gone. You can change your set up statement to take into account your efforts to fix the problem, and your desire for continued progress.

> *"Even though I have some remaining anxiety, I deeply and completely accept myself."*
> *"Even though I'm still a little worried about this interview, I deeply and completely accept myself."*

And so on.

- Now that you've focused on dispelling your immediate anxiety, you can work on installing some positive feelings instead.

Radical acceptance

A few years ago, one Christmas Eve, rather than being at home, being a good wife and a loving mother, I left home. I ditched the kids and abandoned my husband who was baking in the kitchen and I ran all over town until I found a tattoo artist who could ink me. Without question or doubt, I knew that this was the day I had to get these words tattooed on my body. This day I needed it to be part of my being. As my house filled with people, presents and the pressure, I needed a reminder of the "problemlessness" of it all. When I first connected to the question I am about to share with you, it was like something cracked open inside of me to let the light in. I was sitting in my psychologist's office listing off all the things I needed to fix about myself. He looked at me, bemused. When I stopped talking he stared me right in the eye and asked:

What if there is no problem?

The world stopped. Everything since that moment has changed for the better. I couldn't just write this down on a piece of paper. I needed a permanent reminder of this question that would become my personal mantra. I needed to look at this every minute of every day, because for the first time in my life I had a handle on how to get some desperately-needed inner peace. I needed that tattoo as a declaration of personal transformation. The transformation in me came from a simple realisation – *I am not a problem.*

I had been pathologising myself for as long as I could remember. Want the recipe for permanent unhappiness? I had it. I fixated on the belief that, when I sorted out the problem that was me, everything would make sense. I kept myself miserable and suffering for a long time. As a spiritual seeker I was particularly good at using personal development as a weapon of self-destruction. I could identify all my personal failings and the back-story to them with ease. But none of it brought me peace – I was always at odds with myself. In that moment of cracking open, what was concealed for so long became clear. The perfect version of me didn't exist. The need for it kept me from my own happiness. And the problems of my life, well, were they problems? No matter how grievous or painful, or humiliating or shameful, or despairing or enraging my experiences were, they were just life. It was my *story* about them that made them good or bad. When I saw it in that way, I was free to live my life. I was no longer defeated by it. This radical acceptance made me recognise that I wasn't a baking mama. I am an out-getting-tattooed-on-Christmas-Eve mama. This is not the end of the story. As I went deeper into my own self-acceptance, something remarkable happened in my relationship with the world. What if all the problems are not problems?

I noticed that, as observed from this perspective, we are attuned to look at the events of the world as problems. We are entrained into the problemitisation of life. We are taught to measure our reality by what we do not yet have, or that which we have lost. We are not trained to accept that this is just life happening, that good or bad, this too shall pass. When we switch the filter from "problem" to "acceptance", the fear begins to dissipate. I am not suggesting for one minute that the problems stop – they don't stop. In fact, the more awake we become to ourselves, the more aware we are that the problems of the world are endless. But our worry doesn't transform the situation we are experiencing or seeing. It only adds to it. What if I stop seeing problems at all? What just might change the world, just as it changed me, is the shift in perspective. Reducing the world to its problems doesn't let us embrace reality as a continuum of experience. It is life happening. This shift set me free to act. I moved from overwhelm to empowerment, emboldened by my acceptance of what is. In accepting what is, I could take action to make necessary change.

Acceptance of myself was the gateway to my personal peace. Shifting my perspective was as simple as changing my focus. Surrendering judgement is a radical act, but it is possible. I began by letting go of the addiction to judging myself. Next up, I stop judging the world. And perhaps, the peace I found in me can be found out there, too. It is what brought me into behaving in accordance with the law of correspondence. I couldn't see myself as a problem and then be surprised that the world was throwing all the problems at me. I started to use this question as a living practice.

The practice: what if there is no problem?

This practice is almost too simple. Every time you notice a stressful thought, simply ask yourself the question: *What if there is no problem?*

The situation might be problematic, but it is the vibration we hold towards it that will determine if we are adding fuel to the fire or quenching it. We know too well that our worry doesn't resolve our problems and we understand that if we can commit to living in accordance with the law, then in order to change our external reality we need to alter our inner belief. You can also use Byron Katie's question that I adore: *Is that true?* When we start to question the validity of our stressful thoughts, rather than rushing to find evidence to validate the fear, we have the keys to our own liberation in our hands. It is easy to withhold certain life events from the questioning, hiding in the belief that this problem is a *real* problem. There is nothing that is so big that it cannot be transmuted. Radical acceptance of what is, the state of our lives as they are, is the key to creating the change we desire. When we are arguing with the way things are, we are stuck in our victim archetype and are impotent to make change. Byron Katie calls it *loving what is*. It is not condoning or permitting more of the same. It is acknowledging the reality without fear and freeing us and our creative life force to seek alternatives. The questions *What if there is no problem?* and *Is that true?* remove the judgement and, therefore, the fear from our life events. When the fear is removed, and the stress is taken out of the situation – stress that is simply hijacking our intuitive intelligence – we can begin to see the wood for the trees. More importantly, beyond being able to look more logically at a situation, we are able to move out of our heads and back into our hearts, the home of our intuitive intelligence. This is where the miracle-minded moves in, because our vibration is no longer blocking the Infinite's attempts to support us.

Tosha Silver's practice of adding the phrase *without God* to any negative, stress-inducing fear statement instantly reminds

us to come home to our Infinite nature, rather than our limited human nature. This practice is equally simple and as powerful as inquiring into the true nature of our problems. When you hear the negative, "this is impossible" statement, add *without God* to the end:[25]

> *I'll never be free of this debt … without God. I can't hear my intuition … without God.*
> *I'll always meet the wrong kind of partner … without God.*

We come home to our hearts in an instant, and remember we are not doing this thing called life on our own. It is impossible to stay in the low vibration of fear when we use these questions, and when we move out fear, that's when the miracles begin. We come back into alignment with the law.

Imagination is the portal to intuitive intelligence

We're going to really meet our intuitive intelligence when we understand that imagination, and our capacity to imagine, is the portal to our most remarkable life. Many of my students have begun their training decrying their intuition as *just their imagination.* At this point I always stand and cheer, for yes: this is the very gateway to our intuition! Einstein's oft- referenced statement that imagination is more important than knowledge hints at the power of this remarkable capacity, so essential to the full expression of the intuitive intelligence within us. The world we inhabit when we believe only in human reality as perceived through the dominant senses is so limited, so mundane, and such a tiny fragment of all that really is, that without imagination it would be impossible for us to conceive of our own magnificence. And understanding this is another cornerstone of activating our intuitive intelligence. We must imagine ourselves back into our magnificent truth.

Venice Bloodworth explains it this way:

Call on your imagination, the most wonderful power we have, and paint mental pictures of what you want. Build yourself and your environment as you would have them, build them with prayer and thanksgiving and be not anxious as to the results ... It is impossible to see two pictures at the same time.[26]

Imagination is letting go of analytical and conceptual thinking. It is us, present and relaxed. The Infinite wants to create something through us. We are aligned with a very powerful energy stream. It is not fantasising, which is about escape from present time. The key to having confidence in our intuition is like all things outlined in this book. It is about clearing our blocks to trusting our co-creative partner, our intuition and, ergo, our imagination.

There is much written about the intersection between scientific breakthrough and the capacities of the imagination, and this is with good reason. The great scientists often speak of the moment of inspiration that took them from frustration at what they could not see to enlightenment about their next discovery. So, it is with imagination and intuition: a properly-prepared mind will be able to hear the imagination- fuelled language of intuition. Intuition is visual and symbolic. No wonder, then, that the imagination is the bridge that carries intuition insights. When we understand and practice both the techniques of emptying out our subconscious minds and the tools that enhance the muscle of intuition, then we can trust the imagination's offerings. Imagination is a portal. When we resist it, we stymie the flow of our intuition.

Let me explain it further like this: we spiritual folk often talk in the language of dimensions. The third and fifth dimensions are spoken about frequently. What exactly are we talking about? The fifth dimension is pure energy, pure consciousness if you like. The third dimension is solid matter, the world that can be perceived with the five dominant senses. On our path of awakening, we are drawing pure unlimited consciousness into solid form. And how do we do that? What is the bridge? The fourth dimension. The fourth dimension is the imagination dimension through which we translate pure consciousness into solid matter. This is what inspiration is, is it not? The fourth dimension is a bridge built by feeling, thought, and language. We now begin to understand why we must be discerning about where we place our consciousness, and not surrender into fantasy. We must strive to keep our imaginations pure, and we do that by staying present. Fantasy is always an attempt to escape the now. Your thoughts are the currency for your life. How do you want to spend them?

I want to share with you an extended passage about the sacred nature of imagination, from Paul Levy's *God the Imagination*:

*We have so lost touch with the profundity of the imag-
ination that the outer world seems to appear solidified
in form, which is merely reflecting that our imagination
is concretizing. Having lost our acquaintance with the
aesthetics of the imagination, we become "an-aesthetic",
numb to our feelings and cut off from the heart, anes-
thetized from ourselves.*

*Disconnected from the creative organ of the imag-
ination, we lose our sense of aesthetics and our capacity to
appreciate beauty. Instead of symbolizing our experience
so as to creatively express and liberate it, we become
seemingly held captive by a self-reinforcing feedback loop
inside of our minds which continually generates a literal,
particularized, and concretized viewpoint, both towards
the world and ourselves. To the extent that we lose our
connection with the ever-flowing novelty and majesty of
our own creative imagination, we forget our fluid nature,
becoming stunned into immobilization, alienated from
and a trauma to ourselves. The play of and our play with
the creative imagination, however, is the very act that
cultivates, empowers and transfigures the subtle body into
healing nectar, which dissolves and dis-spells our seeming
trauma.*[27]

These words move me to my core. I see within them the
reasons so many of us are so suspicious of our intuitive
knowing, and so wedded to the mind of logic and reason. We
do not live in a time of privileging mysticism (although it is
returning). We have, as Levy writes, become very literal, fixed,
and concretised in our thinking. As such, we have become
fixed in our subconscious minds. Leaning into our intuition
and the symbolic and archetypal patterns of our life can

seem strange and unusual. At different times in our human civilisation this kind of intelligence was privileged. Those who could see readily through the veils to the world within the worlds were sought out and consulted for their wisdom.

When we remember the laws of mentalism and correspondence we can see how powerful a tool imagination is to realise our intuitive intelligence and live our bliss. All is of the mind. If we cannot imagine an alternative to our reality, then how can we make it so? Adhering to the law of correspondence, if we cannot make a state of being real inside of us – for example, feeling the world is loving when we are only seeing fear – how can we bring about that loving world? We must imagine it first to bring the conditions into being that will make it real. The result of losing imagination, as Levy goes on to say, is we become numb to ourselves and to our world. This only deepens our belief in separation and isolation. "We are alienated from and a trauma to ourselves," says Levy, and when we approach this statement from the perspective of the law of correspondence, we can understand why.

Our numbness within is generating a numb, yet traumatic, world outside of us. We accept without question the dominant paradigm and fear it cannot be any other way. Worst of all is that when divine revelation visits us, we reject it for we fear it, and fear ourselves. We do not understand what our intuition is saying, and we cannot bear the paradox, the mystery, so literal have we become in our meaning-making. The intuitively intelligent amongst us make peace with the paradox and enter willingly into the mystery of our existence. We let the symbols of our intuition roll over us, knowing that what we need to know will appear in concrete form when the time is right. Until then, the play between the subconscious and the God mind does its work preparing us for the life of our highest design. If we continue to reject the capacities of our imagination, we reject our greatest creative role, which is to create our own lives. And we reject our co-creative partner, the Infinite.

The law of correspondence is the acceptance of radical personal power. It can be brought into action only through the discipline of spiritual fierceness. We cannot hide from ourselves. We are creating the conditions of our life, and we understand we are creating from within. What is within necessarily must be in accordance with what we desire to see outside in the world. There is nowhere to hide in this. There is only the great power of realising our unlimited selves.

Chapter 5

The Law Of Vibration

The law of vibration will really take hold in our life when we remember that love is all there is. This principle explains the difference between the different manifestations of matter and spirit, or how in reality there is no difference. Every atom and molecule is vibrating in a certain motion, speed, vibration, and frequency. Science has been telling us for more than a hundred years now that everything is energy, and that we are part of a unified consciousness, or quantum field. We have not taken this knowledge on as a society, I believe, because it terrifies us. With great power comes great responsibility. What if I am one with all that there is, and not only that, but my vibration is informing Infinite consciousness and telling it how to behave? This is indeed what the law of vibration points to. I am literally manufacturing my existence through my consciousness. As we know from the levels of mind, most of our consciousness is subconscious, which is why it seems like the world is not showing up as we want it to, and instead in the form of what we are most afraid of. We are setting matter into motion through our consciousness. Our consciousness contains the vibration of our feeling state. The ideal is to create a motion that is determined by our Higher Self, rather than by the lower self, or negative ego.

This law is this statement in action:

Energy first, physical second.

As Gregg Braden states in *Resilience from the Heart*:

The bottom line is we're bathed in a field of energy that's everywhere, always present, and one that existed since time began with the Big Bang. The existence of this field implies three principles that have a direct effect upon the way we live, all that we do, and the role of our heart in our lives.

Braden goes on to state that the first principle "suggests that because everything exists within a matrix of energy, everything is connected. It's this connection that makes deep states of intuition between people and patterns between significant life events possible."[28] This is exactly what my book postulates, and what the law of vibration promises. The next two principles have already been introduced in the previous laws: the holographic nature of that unifying energy field, and the intimate union of past, present, and future. No matter how it appears through the dominant senses, quantum physics confirms that we are not solid matter at all. Our belief in ourselves as solid matter is one of the greatest impediments to our intuitive intelligence, and this law is the way to unlock our consciousness. Literally, our consciousness is vibration, and if we want to change our reality, we need to change our feeling state. The Kybalion puts it this way:

Every thought, emotion or mental state has its corresponding rate and mode of vibration. And by an effort of the will of the person, or of other persons, these mental states may be reproduced, just as a musical tone may be reproduced by causing an instrument to vibrate at a certain rate – just as colour may be reproduced in the same may. By a knowledge of the Principle of Vibration, as applied to Mental Phenomena, one may polarize his mind at any degree he wishes, thus gaining a perfect control over his mental states, moods, etc.[29]

Mastery of this law means forgoing the belief we are limited victims of circumstance. The quantum field, which we are calling God, is impartial and waiting for us to decide. What we are learning is that the language of the quantum field is vibration. What sets particles of matter in motion, into vibration, is our feeling state. Our feeling state is generated by the following formula that I learnt from Gregg Braden:

Thought + emotion = feeling.

Let me illustrate this for you. The thought can be anything. Without emotion, the thought is innocent. It's coming from our reasoning conscious mind. Let's say:

I'm going to start my own business.

The thought sets in motion an emotional response, remembering that the emotional response will be coming from our subconscious mind. All our emotions are one of two things: love or fear. This vision for our life, the thought *I'm going to start my own business*, triggers the emotion of fear. In that subconscious mind, all the stories of fear of failure, self-doubt, and humiliation rush up to meet that innocent thought. The next step is where we break the law and wonder why our lives don't look like the vision we are holding for them. The emotion meets the thought in the heart, which is the location of communication with the Infinite or quantum field. It generates a feeling and feeling carries a vibration. That feeling is thought meeting emotion, and the feeling is fearful. So, we either quash our idea before it has even begun, or if we do step out on the path we fail, because what we set in motion is in accordance with our vibration.

What sets energy in motion is not our thoughts and not our emotions, but the sum of both those things moving out into the Infinite through the intuitive intelligence centre, the heart. The heart is the communication centre. God is love, therefore our greatest and only aim is to hold the vibration of love. Therefore, we need to move beyond mindfulness and beyond the idea that thoughts create things, which is simply not the case. The mind is a step in the process, but it is the heart that programs reality. We do not need to hold our thoughts on a thing; hence the reason affirmations don't work for most of us. It is essential that we understand consciousness communicates through the feeling state, and as such we need to master our feelings. We need to come into the highest vibration we can. As the law of vibration states, every feeling has a corresponding rate and mode of vibration. We do not need to watch every thought. We need to learn how to operate from our heart. The heart is the location of our intuitive intelligence because it is where our consciousness resides, and where our individuated consciousness connects to the Infinite consciousness. What this law requires of us is to surrender belief in the solidness of our lives – our finite selves, or the permanence of matter. Luckily for us, quantum physics is a powerful way to see beyond solid form into our true nature. Planck time is a powerful example of this. Max Planck was the first scientist to propose this concept. Author Brandon West explains Planck time and the law of vibration:

> *Because reality is flashing in and out of existence (hypothetically at Planck time – 10^{30} times per second) … every time our reality oscillates between form, and the pure energy state of the field, our awareness – which is constant and doesn't flash in and out of existence – informs the field what to reappear as when it makes its transition back to form at the quantum level. Therefore, each time we oscillate into formlessness, we have complete and total control and responsibility over what we choose with our attention to manifest out of the field in the next moment, and our power and ability to do so relies entirely [on] what we believe, and on how we are feeling. (https://www.wakingtimes.com/2014/04/16/ proof-human-body-projection-consciousness/)*

When we begin to master this law, we do not do it with the mind. We must go beyond mental concepts into a mastery of the feeling state so that we can operate from the site of our consciousness – the heart. The Infinite is only love. Love is the highest vibration. We cannot know love, we can only experience it. And when we do, we see the miracles unfold. This is what happened for me when I faced the greatest fear of them all: the fear of death.

The Third turning point

Archetype: Wild woman/Crone
Mantra: Silence
Intuition type: Visionary

What is it to sit with your mother hours before her open-heart surgery and know that you are not afraid that she might die? That you have completely surrendered the need for her to live or to die? To be fearless in the face of the mortality of the woman you love most in the world? For me it was sweet revelation. It was coming home. It was, in many ways, my beginning. In March 2017, my mother was admitted to hospital at, as one doctor described it, "five minutes to midnight". Her heart was in a very bad way. She was such a high risk of having a heart attack at any moment that at one point she was not allowed even to leave her bed to use the bathroom. This sudden turn of events was in fact many years in the making. The downturn of my mother's health had been concerning to me for some time, but no doctor could help her. Then my father came down with a virus and was bed-bound, meaning my mother took on more of the manual labour than usual. That's when the problem escalated, and she was hospitalised with chest pain. A tiny vein pumping blood between the left and right sides of her heart, it turns out, was the only thing keeping her alive.

When I flew into her hometown to be with her prior to her surgery, she was the most serene I had seen her in a long time. Perhaps through relief at finally knowing why all her symptoms, previously undiagnosed, existed, and perhaps at the possibility of a life that was not ruled by pain and exhaustion. Several days later, as I sat alone with her in her hospital room on the eve of her surgery, something shifted. She looked at me with tears in her eyes and spoke of her fear. This was an epic surgery, a triple bypass, and high-risk. She had never tolerated anaesthetic well and was weak because of the weeks of prior "turns" that included collapsing on the ferry that took her to her island home. I could feel the power of her fear. In that moment, I was overtaken with an experience of grace that altered me. I knew I could surrender her to the Infinite knowing that nothing would change. Her true nature would not be touched, no matter if she were incarnate or not. And I knew – although I was not asked to test that knowing – that I would not grieve her. How could I? She is me, not because she is my mother, but because she is the same stuff that I am. Infinite, unlimited consciousness. And death simply does not exist.

All my life had led me to this moment, where I could sit unafraid before the thing that previously would have scared me most, and that I could hold that state of grace so that my beloved mother could experience it, too. It is one thing to surrender attachment to our own lives. I had done that the year before when I had come close to death at a retreat I was attending. There was a fire in our compound and, whilst no one was hurt, I am told that as we ran from the fire a live power line missed me by millimetres. This information and the event of the fire also did not surprise me. For the days leading up to this event I had been repeating a prayer to myself:

Even this life, God, if you want it, it is yours.

I had realised that most of our fear lies in our belief in the finality of death, this most ultimate of acts of separation from a human perspective and, as such, the most powerful belief to surrender. As we move along the path of spiritual awakening, we become more and more prepared to surrender the things of the world, for we know that they are not the cause of our peace. God is. But we remain quite stubbornly attached to the idea of life. We believe that death is an end because most of us have not seen beyond it and returned to tell the tale. As I entered that retreat I was prepared to offer myself up in this way, because I knew my ego was still motivating so many of my actions in the world. I still believed that success, for example, would bring me happiness. I still believed that my power was out there in the world, or in what the world reflected back to me. I could not think of a more efficient exercise than to surrender attachment to this human life as a way to overcome the ego's attachment. I didn't expect quite such an epic sign that God was listening. The fire didn't harm me, but it had another unexpected and magnificent side effect. As I stood defenceless before God and offered my life, I was shown how frail and vulnerable this human form is.

I was also blessed with an experience of grace so profound that it altered me forever. In that moment of running in the dark from the fire I experienced *shaktipat*. The spiritual author Gabriel Cousens describes *shaktipat* as "the awakening of the Divine force that is resting in potential within us. This is known as the descent of Grace. It usually occurs through a living, enlightened spiritual leader, but may occur spontaneously."[31] In that moment, I was initiated into my wild woman. With experience of the descent of grace I felt fearless. What is wilder than to be without fear? I could feel my wild heart as all that I feared melted away – fear of failure, fear of humiliation, fear of death – as the grace pulsated through me.

By the time I sat before my mother, and witnessed her own moment of facing death, I knew I was being initiated into the archetype of the crone. My clients will often say to me that it is not their own death that they fear most, but the death of their families. Yet, the crone draws closer to the veil between the worlds. She has lost attachment to the external. Her presence is slow and still, for she is listening, not adding more noise to the world. She has seen the cycle of birth and death, and she has forgone the doubt that plagued her in her youth. She is spiritual fierceness in action. By the time I sat with my mother on the eve of her surgery, the need for words was over. Finally, silence imbued with grace was between these two restless spiritual seekers. The vibration that moved between us carried the message, and the message was wordless, formless, love. What attachment could I possibly have to life when we had this? Caroline Myss says that visionary intuition is the final initiation. It is total surrender to the Infinite. Visionary intuition is when we allow effortless passage to the vision of God that wants to appear through us. We don't cling to our own agenda. We surrender to our unlimited selves. I could not know what the outcome of my mother's operation would be, but I did know that I would trust and love with my whole being whatever the outcome was.

Not surprisingly, given her willingness and mine to accept whatever outcome, she came through the surgery with flying colours. We were both initiated into our sacred hearts on the eve of her open-heart surgery, and the metaphor was not lost on us. We returned to a state of love, the highest vibration of all, which also explains why intuitive intelligence resides in the heart. The very point of understanding the law of vibration is to understand that we want to raise our vibration, or in other words, the capacity to know and hold the feeling state of love above all else.

Intuitive intelligence is a divine feminine power (and a female power too)

The mystical woman is the ultimate wild woman.
— Sally Lakshmi Thurley

For 8000 years, since the beginning of the decimation of the goddess cultures, women have been slowly reduced in power, authority, connection, value, and place. An article in the British newspaper, *The Independent*, shows clearly that it has not always been this way:

A distinct pattern is discernible from the evidence that has been left by these early civilisations. Stretching from the ancient Indus Valley, right across the mountains of Anatolia, to the islands of the Mediterranean and as far as the topmost island of Orkney in Scotland, what emerges is a series of like-minded civilisations whose temples and graves bear witness to a lifestyle of peace and a veneration for mother nature. Their common belief in the continuous cycle of birth, death, and regeneration is personified by their worship of a mother goddess in all her forms: snake, vulture, pregnant woman or moon. Excellence in craftwork, technical skill and exquisite art are some of their legacies, along with a spirit of natural equality. This was not to continue. During the second millennium BC, the last of these early civilisations fell. New power in the form of military might was sweeping across Europe, the Middle East and Asia. Warriors had worked out how to prey off the profits of others, ushering in an age when human elitism, ruthlessness and terror had their true beginnings[32].

This cycle of reducing the power of women has been slowly changing since the last century (with a few moments of resurgence in the last several thousand years also). We are beginning to reclaim our political rights, our economic rights, and our domestic rights. We are reclaiming everything in the human reality. This is vital work, and it is the precursor to where we are now. Now, we need to reclaim our spiritual power. We battle as an entire civilisation with the imbalance between divine masculine and divine feminine, this division the perfect metaphor for the soul-destroying duality that rules the planet at this time. The predominant separation of this age is our separation from the divine feminine.

Time has eroded the knowing of this innate sense in the human being. And I do not simply mean the time of our life since our birth. These last 8000 years have brought a systematic and singularly successful eradication of *wild knowing* in the hearts and minds of every single person who has lived. From more than 8000 years ago when the warring tribes of Asia moved across the globe and merged, married, or murdered the goddess in all her forms, to the contemporary age where the "invisible" patriarchy sanctioned the commodification of the female form so that it is almost impossible for a woman to think of herself as anything but a mechanism of pleasure and beauty for men, the separation of humanity from its very nature has been complete. But it is not absolute. It can't be, because the creator, our divine nature, resides within us. Women live in a paradigm that reduces our worth every single day. We must change our perspective from the outer world, and its imbalanced representation of the divine feminine, and take our sight inwards to our mystical natures. Whenever a woman begins to wake up she automatically becomes a healer, a teacher, and a leader for her community.

Creating community and coherence is a divine feminine power. The role of the awakening Priestess is vital to the health of the world and to the communities in which they live. Gathering the energy of the circle to bring all into power is the way of the feminine power.

The divine feminine is the seat of the sacred. And so, as a civilisation we are suspicious, cynical, and often violent towards to the sacred mysteries, including our own intuitive power. We simply have been so long estranged from this power that we cannot recognise it as our own. We are terrified of its potency, so we seek to suppress it further with our intellect and doubt. Our self-doubt becomes our obsession, rather than wondering what is on the other side of it. It is a smoke screen. We cannot claim what we do not remember is our own innate nature – we are lost to ourselves. Yet restoring this balance, overcoming the illusion of duality, will make it possible to awaken the divine communion. Intuition is a receptive skill. It is associated with the feminine aspect of our nature, with all our natures, for we are all – men and women – made up of the feminine and masculine. Intuition is receptive, and that simply means that we must open and allow ourselves to receive it. It cannot be forced to reveal itself. It is why meditation, the ultimate receptive act of the spiritual seeker, is a cornerstone of awakening intuition. We open to it.

This is my belief: we are born into female form because we are willing to be the mystics, the keepers of the mysteries. We are the portal to the divine. When our soul chooses to incarnate into the female form it is because we have agreed to be the holders of the divine feminine power. The divine feminine power has been so deeply maligned that we do not even realise that we continue to subjugate ourselves before the masculine. The power differential is thus because we have been told for thousands of years that we are *less than*. The jealousy, suspicion, and fear of the sacred mysteries, of the receptive power of the divine feminine in this current historical cycle, has placed the woman – as well as the divine feminine – to the *lesser than* category. We have been led to believe that there is something wrong with women, so the self- esteem of the woman at the individual and collective level is in ruins. Until we right that, we will be the victims of our own lives. When we begin talking about ourselves as the vortex of sacred power, then we will truly be making a paradigm shift, in which the woman will be revered, be worshipped. For she is the direct access to the divine. We have devalued our spirituality, our soul nature as a civilisation, and as such we have demoted those who are the most directly connected to the divine.

We are not just suspicious of divine feminine power, we as women are taught to be suspicious of power in each other. Now, instead, we are called to unite as a sisterhood, and raise one another up, to create spaces in which it is safe to speak of our wild intuitive knowing. When we give up our suspicion of one another, which has been culturally indoctrinated by this imbalance, we heal the wounding of millennia. We will restore peace to the world. That change happens at the level of the soul. Intuitive intelligence is divine feminine power. It is receptive power, in which the knowing enters you. It is not hunted down or sought out. It comes to you when you open yourself to it. It is the paradigm of "do without doing, and everything gets done". It is not the domain of women alone, for each of us contains the polarity of feminine and masculine divine. Whilst the feminine in physical form on earth is reduced, abused, beaten, broken, neglected, and devalued then we can say with certainty this is what we are also doing to our divine natures.

How does receptive power work? How can we sit back and receive what we need? Divine feminine power is so lost to the world that the idea of surrender – the root of receptive power – is extremely threatening to most. When I speak about surrender to my students it is often met with blank stares, even though we throw the word about very casually in spiritual circles. We know the idea is good, and we should be doing more of it if we want to get closer to our Infinite natures, but what does it involve? Surrender is in fact *trust*. We cannot surrender if we do not trust that the Infinite is there to catch us. Likewise, we cannot access receptive power if we are suspicious or doubtful that what we need will come to us. We simply have not been raised, for many generations, as witnesses to this kind of power, so it seems impossible. We don't believe at our core the central tenet of intuitive intelligence – *I am a divine piece of a benevolent God that is always working on my behalf.* We must begin with a shift in perspective: nothing outside of us needs to change. We need to give ourselves permission to determine our own life. Self-determination is key. We need to consent to ourselves that we are worthy. To increase our intuition, we need to hold ourselves in high esteem.

It is important to note that whilst I am advocating for the special access women have to intuitive intelligence, it is not really a gendered capacity at all. The weight of the historical narrative of the last several thousand years, however, has made it very difficult for us as a civilisation to value the qualities of the divine feminine, or simply feminine, especially those born into the female body. As such, those born into male bodies have inherited a lot of programming that in most cases prevents men in our world today seeing value in embodying the divine feminine within them. There are many exceptions, however until there is a cultural shift as there is beginning to be, on a worldwide scale, men will not take the steps to understand the power of the divine feminine because they simply don't need to. The world is built to respect and reward masculine power, and many of those born into women's bodies have learnt to imitate it.

These words will not sit well with many. I understand that we take these kinds of ideas very personally and leap to defend our own men, brothers, and sons rather than sitting with the discomfort of the collective unconscious and archetypal imbalance. Globally, there is a crisis that has been happening for thousands of years, a crisis in which women are the possessions and objects of a male-centric world. But it has not always been this way. And the first step in the return to balance is to shore up the weaker side. At this time, that is the divine feminine, for it has been so long abused that we – as the inheritors of the wounds inflicted – need additional scaffolding.

When the balance returns, the intuitive intelligence of all will rise again, and we will occupy in equal parts the Shiva and Shakti, or masculine and feminine, within. This balance is the return to union, or oneness, in which gender does not exist as a measure of anything. It just is, and one cannot exist without the other.

Energy first

Intuitive intelligence is a symptom, one of awakening consciousness. It is a symptom of recognising that we are more than our physical bodies. We are energy moving through space – some of that energy has solidified and taken on the form of the human body, and some of it is less dense and more moveable, and this we call the energy body. When we accept ourselves as this combination of dense matter and energy body we begin to address our own needs in a completely different way. We understand that our subtle or energy anatomy requires care and nourishment in the same way that our physical bodies do. Our health, the quality of our lives, and the depth of our intuitive intelligence is all determined by understanding our energy anatomy. As Caroline Myss explains in *Anatomy of the Spirit*:

> *Everything that is alive pulsates with energy and all of this energy contains information ... your physical body is surrounded by an energy field that extends as far out as your outstretched arms and the full length of your body. It is both an information centre and a highly sensitive perceptual system. We are constantly in communication with everything around us through this system.*[33]

Once we understand that we are energy and that we are communicating all the time from this place, then we can begin that communication. In other words, we can change the story. This is a process called resonance. When people greet you in a particular way it is because you've already energetically shaken their hand or hugged them, or maybe even given them a shove depending on how you feel about them. That much more expansive, invisible part of you is conducting your life for you. You don't know why others respond to you in the way they do, and you don't know why certain situations go your way and then others don't.

You are emitting powerful signals all the time out into the world, and the world is responding. This is a huge revelation. You are so much more than you realised, and you can influence your environment so much more powerfully than you ever knew. Resonance is accessed through a variety of practices – including the ones described in this book – that return the body to its coherent state. We can also call this entraining to the Divine. We are unifying our energy or light body with the frequency or resonance of unity, oneness, God.

When we operate from intuitive intelligence, communicating and listening from this place, we become more peaceful and relaxed. We feel supported and guided. We feel like we are in partnership with the Infinite. We are accessing the part of ourselves that is holding the highest vibration. That is because we are letting life work on our behalf rather than forcing it into action. In regard to resonance, we hold the highest vibration and then we get out of the way and let the Infinite go to work.

The practice: chanting

As sound is vibration, it makes sense that one of the most immediate and powerful ways to up-level our vibration is to *sound*. Listening to music instantly changes our mood. Rather than this being coincidental, the reality is that we are altering our vibration by using music we love to change our feeling state. The act of sounding – in this case chanting – works in the same way, yet even more powerfully. And why is that? When we chant sacred sounds, such as ancient mantras, we are repeating sounds that have been uttered in reverence billions of times before. We are attuning to the vibration of the utterance of that sound in all directions of time and space. It takes us out of our cranial brain and into the feeling state very quickly.

There are many chants you can work with. I am sharing with you one of my favourites because it is so simple, and because it builds in tempo so that you can experience the sensation bodily of raising your vibration through sound. So*ham* is a Hindu mantra, meaning, "I am He/That" in Sanskrit. In Vedic philosophy, it means identifying oneself with the Infinite, or ultimate reality. *I am that I am* is an often-uttered spiritual mantra, so even though this is a Hindu mantra, the meaning is transcendent. We are aligning ourselves with/as God as we chant.

You can find my version here: https://instituteforintuitiveintelligence.com/justforyou

To use this sound without the chant, simply repeat it to yourself as often as you like. Or you may simply use the English translation *I am that I am*, which is the response that God used in the Hebrew Bible when Moses asked for his name (Exodus 3:14). It is one of the most famous verses in the Torah.

Your vibration is your protection

What is it to be protected when we live life with intuitive intelligence? The idea of protection refers to the belief prevalent in much spiritual doctrine that we need to keep ourselves energetically clear of other people's energy, and in particular those people who are perceived to be holding lower vibrational frequencies than us. It is not limited to people, however. In this kind of belief, we are as equally vulnerable to non-incarnate entities and places. What does this mean? Some people and places don't feel good to us, and others feel downright scary. Some people and places appear to drain us and leave us feeling exhausted and overwhelmed.

We may find ourselves saying, "the vibe was off" or "that person didn't gel with me". In these cases, we are experiencing something energetically that feels out of alignment, without necessarily knowing what is happening. We may learn to stay away from those people and places, although more often than not this is not possible, or we do not have enough faith in our feeling or knowing to back ourselves up. Instead, much new age philosophy will recommend visualising yourself in a bubble, separating yourself energetically from the things, people, and places you feel are bringing you down, vibrationally speaking (and it's all vibration).

These practices teach us a myriad of external tools to release the low vibes. Intuitive intelligence is a practice predicated on a return to oneness, union with the one mind. I posit a radically different position, one that I believe is vital to the success of being the most intuitively intelligent that is possible: it is our job as leaders of the spiritually fierce movement to overcome the belief in separation. Our power is in determining how we receive other people's energy. We walk around believing we are vulnerable to the world. We don't remember that this physical body is simply an extension of our energetic body. We have a choice about the energy we project into the world through resonance. When we remember this, we change the way we talk about energetic protection and, more importantly, the way in which we participate in our own lives. When we go into the world, or a meeting, or a client session believing we need to "protect" ourselves, we are invested in the illusion of separation. Instead we can approach it like this:

I prepare the environments, people and myself by holding the highest vibration possible. I set the intention for all by holding the vibration of compassion in my own energy field.

Scientists can measure the electromagnetic field of human beings. It extends about 2.5 metres from the body. Why is our field this big? Well, that's because the instruments that measure the field cannot read beyond that! The truth is our fields are vast, and high vibrational – or coherent – states such as gratitude, compassion, and appreciation increase the power and potency of the field. Our field is joined to the Infinite field, and so to alter our experiences, to "protect" our piece of the field, we simply need to increase our vibration. Three minutes of Heart Congruence before entering our day, before entering a shopping centre, before anything at all, will ensure the highest possible outcome not only for ourselves, but for all, because we are coming into resonance with the vibration we want to be experiencing.

If I believe I need to separate myself from others in order to survive the low vibrations of the world, then I am contributing to that low vibration. But if I make it my service to take my vibration so high each day that, no matter where I am, I am contributing that frequency to all those around me, then I have changed the world for good. When I hold this quality of vibration in my daily life, then something very interesting starts to happen: all those around me will respond. My life will come into coherence or congruence, where the external matches my internal state. My higher vibrational state is an offer. The people in my life will either take that offer and we all move into coherence together, or they fall away from my life. If they fall away, then I know that those people, events, places etc. were simply not in coherence with the frequency of my life. Nothing is lost. And I have my "protection".

Discernment

This kind of protection is an act of sacred service, supporting all to return to oneness. Together we rise beyond the illusion of separation. This kind of protection also supports our discernment. Those people we see as a problem are us. Do we want them to suffer by excluding them from our love? *No.* Does that mean we want to spend time with those people or places that are not in coherence with us? The answer to that is also *no.* Our love for them as an aspect of us does not make us personally responsible for the world. It makes us personally responsible for ourselves. And discernment is an excellent tool for the intuitively intelligent person to apply. Just as we must be vigilant to keep our vibration high and light, we must work for our discernment. As Meggan Watterson offers:

> *Discernment can be difficult. Often there is a lot of spiritual sweat involved, because we're not ready to see what, in fact, the soul is clearly showing us we need to do. We create aversions and distractions, and we flail around as if we're drowning, or we pretend that we're lost.*[34]

We know that this is the very heart of what it is to be intuitively intelligent – to act upon what the soul is clearly showing us we need to do. It is easier – and here is the temptation of the idea of protection – to blame something outside of us as the reason we have been led into the lower vibrations. An energetic "entity" for example, or our housemate's "bad vibes", a helpful conjunction of planets, or a crystal with a "negative" energy attached to it. The victim archetype will search desperately outside of themselves for the cause of their suffering. I am enormously frustrated by the cries of those who identify as empaths and highly-sensitive people who act in this way, making claims that allow people to opt out of life in myriad ways. All seven billion of us are highly sensitive. We are electro-magnetic beings emitting waves of information constantly. This is part of our superpower toolkit that we largely ignore or misinterpret as a kind of rare and precious disability. It is part of the "aversions and distractions" that Watterson speaks of. In the same way that having constant emotional turmoil in our lives is an excellent excuse to not show up to our intuitive intelligence, believing we are vulnerable and separate keeps us out of our power.

When I am in coherence, I am clear on what vibes with me and who I want to spend my time with, where I want to spend my time, and what kind of things I want to be doing with my time. I make choices from this place of radical self-love rather than a place of clouded confusion and fear. I am not only in resonance with the vibration I want to be living through, I am generating that vibration. I am literally raising the vibration for myself and all around me. I am no longer passively receiving life. When we are operating from our intuitive intelligence, our heart's intuitive knowing guides our choices. This discernment will become second nature and an effortless choice, because the more we devote to holding our vibration in a coherent state, the more difficult it is to inhabit lower vibrational states for any length of time.

The practice: energetic protection

In addition to the practice of Heart Congruence, one of the most powerful tools for "energetic protection" is the following visualisation. Please remember, we are not really protecting anything. The belief required for intuitive intelligence to flourish is:

I am a divine piece of a benevolent God that is always working on my behalf.

As the law of correspondence shows us, whatever is in the world around me is simply corresponding to my inner world and, not only that, but doing this in service to my awakening so I may overcome this faulty belief. The law of mentalism has lovingly guided us to the truth that all is one, so if I invoke the idea of "protection", I am in fear and lowering my consciousness.

Let me be very clear here: if you believe you need protection, your need for protection will be made so. It is a lose/lose situation to believe we need protecting. The only protection possible is in the central belief of intuitive intelligence. Then we must trust the events of our life, and trust the intuitive knowing that is always guiding us so that we are in flow with our highest good. Not only will we make more discerning choices based on our intuitive intelligence regarding where we want to spend our time and with whom, we will also not see threat in any person, place or thing. We will only see love, for love is all there is. That perception will guide us towards situations, people and events that are in alignment with the highest vibration It can be difficult to remember this in the moment, especially when we are in fear, so here's a visual that will take you there:

Before you are in the presence of someone who "drains" you, or need to go to a place that feels out of alignment with you (such as a shopping centre, or a government office, or whatever it is for you), or any variation on this thinking imagine the entire place, person, thing elevated by orbs of lights. If it is a person you feel threatened by, for example, see yourself and that person with arms outstretched. Under each arm is a magnificent ball of light. The colour doesn't matter – let your imagination show you what it will. As you observe these orbs of light, notice yourself and the other rising higher and higher off the ground. See the effortless grace of the light as it takes you high into the Infinite. Nothing can touch you here. All fear melts away like butter melting in the sun.

Will this prevent anything "bad" from ever happening to you? This is, ultimately, a redundant question. Instead, think of it like this: will it support you to overcome the belief in duality? In good and bad? To make discerning, divinely inspired choices, even if they seem illogical or even impolite? *Yes.* Surrendering judgment may the hardest thing we have to do as souls having a human experience, but it is entirely possible when we live from intuitive intelligence. It is the highest form of protection.

Solitude and Stillness

At a particularly crazy moment in my life, when there were too many deadlines and not enough time, the inner guru in me was demanding that I head off on retreat. I was craving solitude, and for good reason. I had so much I wanted to be learning, so many new books coming across my desk, podcasts, online training videos, amazing wisdom from every direction. I wanted to be alone with this in deep reverence with my soul. Instead, it was the first week of the school holidays here in Melbourne, and my two boys were not sleeping through the night, nor were they getting on very well with each other. It was the opposite of the retreat I was craving!

The bigger part of me knew that my children were offering me exactly what I needed right then, and life was and always is just as it should be. The yearning simply made me more inventive about how to get that inner retreat. So, I made myself a retreat in my daily life plan.

Why do we even need the idea of retreat? What do we gain from withdrawing from the world? Well, the language of our soul – our intuition – is subtle, and we need to tune into a particular frequency to maximise our access to this highest or deepest part of ourselves. That frequency? Stillness. And it doesn't have to be outward stillness, necessarily. Climbing a mountain for example or doing yoga can be some of the most inward stilling experiences we can have. Stillness is the state of being we want to acquire in order to manage the stress of the world. And the benefits? Innumerable! But let's name a few:

- Emotional regulation – in other words, our capacity to moderate our emotions with inner stillness before unleashing them (or not) on the world.
- Reduction in stress-producing hormones, including adrenaline and cortisol.
- Increase in divergent thinking – an improved capacity to solve problems with ease and creativity.
- An increase in the spontaneous experience of grace.

In addition to all those amazing benefits we can add better sleep and peace of mind, and a reduction in anxiety and renewed energy can be added to the list.

How can we access the benefits of retreating in our busy, child-filled, job- demanding everyday reality? The truth is that the awakening of our souls happens in and through the world, not in spite of it. The world is our training ground, and we have everything we need to thrive. The world is not working against us, it is our active creation, and it is working overtime to come into alignment with what we are asking of it through our vibration.

The practices of solitude and stillness

I don't have just one practice here, but several. All of these can be readily integrated into the normal action of our day-to-day, especially when we are being discerning about where we focus our precious consciousness. For me, all these practices are part of my every day because I have given away things that don't serve me but have traditionally been time suckers. I don't watch television, for example. I simply don't have the time, and there is nothing I could view that is worthwhile to me. Instead I give my consciousness time to breathe with the following tools, which also work very powerfully to show us the contents of our subconscious:

Spend time in contemplation. This isn't mediation but a more active form of inner reflection, which is complemented by making a list of "next steps", or qualities you would like to include in your life. When you make this space open but structured, you find your inner light becomes very bright as you begin to map the future of your life from a place of intuitive intelligence. You are attuning your focus with spiritual fierceness.

Read the sacred texts. It doesn't matter where you begin, or what religion or philosophy you follow, but find the books that inspire your soul and spend at least ten minutes reading from one or more. I have a stack of books beside my bed and I allow myself to gravitate towards whatever I need. As I write this book, I have *A Course in Miracles, The Power of Now, Thinking Like the Universe, The Surrender Experiment* and *Reveal.* It sounds like a long list, but I am actively reading all of them as I am guided to do so. We must keep our consciousness entrained to that which we want to embody. Reading sacred texts is one of the simplest tools to do this. You are using your conscious mind as the access point to the subconscious mind and holding your consciousness on the vibrational set point you want to live.

Have a journal with you all the time or beside your bed. You may find ideas or inspiring thoughts appear from nowhere about your next steps, a problem you may be having, or divine guidance. Believe me, if you don't write it down you will forget it. This is the other side of reading inspirational texts, and a great activity to do alongside contemplation.

And finally, walk. Yes, walk. There is a reason so many of the great pilgrimages on the planet are long, long walks. Walking is such a profound peace-giving activity. It gives you mental, emotional, and spiritual clarity, and in no small way this is because you are silently communing with mother earth. Don't listen to music and don't worry if it is just around the streets of your neighbourhood. Give yourself as much time as you can, ideally at dawn or dusk, and you will find profound inner peace.

Gratitude and forgiveness: Stepping into mastery

Radical gratitude is a technique that you can practice bringing your life into alignment with your highest dreams. Radical gratitude is going beyond making mental lists of what you know you are grateful for (even if some days it is harder to make that list than others). We all know by now that gratitude is where it is at for bringing our lives into full health, wealth, and happiness. What's the difference, though, between the peo2ple who live with an attitude of gratitude all the time, and the ones who are just painfully going through the motions of gratitude list-making because it seems like a good thing to do? The difference is simple, and it is this: living in a state of gratitude is about the feelings that are generated in your heart when you feel grateful for your life, your cup of coffee, the sunshine, the client who cancelled at the last minute, the heavy traffic, the smile on your baby's face. Lots of contradictions in there, right? And here's why: gratitude isn't an external thing at all. To feel gratitude, *really* feel it, you don't need anything outside of you to change. It's okay to begin to live gratitude in a perfunctory, list-making way, especially when life is hard and challenging. Eventually, if you are focussed on this practice, something miraculous will happen – you will internally generate the feeling of gratitude without any external stimulus at all. You will be feeling the grace of gratitude move through you with every breath. This is radical gratitude. I am in profound, radical gratitude for every bit of my life. And in that state, my life has moved gracefully even more in alignment with the life of my dreams.

It is even more powerful to feel gratitude for what is not in alignment. This strongly aligns with radical acceptance. Until we can get on board with how our lives are in the present moment, we are at war with ourselves. Gratitude is not a light and fluffy practice. It takes spiritual fierceness to accept things as they are, and that is achieved by gratitude. Gratitude for things that are less than ideal means accepting our personal power. It also means trusting the Infinite. From our present local and limited human perspective, it may seem impossible to be grateful for certain events of our life. As was mentioned when we discussed radical acceptance, we may fear that we are condoning the things we don't want. But the opposite is true. Gratitude is a feeling state that sets energy in motion at a very high vibration.

That vibration sets the Infinite into motion and the result is more high vibration, not more of the actual, specific events that you are unhappy with. Living with an attitude of gratitude, no matter the external circumstances, is the key to a successful life. It's kind of backwards to how we think it should be. This is the answer to your dreams, though. Feel the gratitude and watch the life of your dreams appear before you.

The practice: radical gratitude

- Sit comfortably. Close your eyes.
- Breathe in through the nose and out through the mouth, releasing with a sigh three times. Take your attention to the centre of your chest and imagine your breath moving in and out from here.
- Bring to mind something you are readily grateful for. Pick something easy and positive.
- Focus on this thing/person/place for two whole minutes, really connecting to the gratitude you feel for it/him/her. Don't stop until you can feel the gratitude throughout your entire chest.
- Now let go of the subject of your gratitude and let the feeling in your chest spread out across your body. Do this by imagining the feeling as an energy that is filling a balloon around you. Fill the balloon with the feeling of gratitude, beyond all proportion to your original mental image. In other words, let this feeling consume you, like a fire.
- Take a deep breath and open your eyes.

Do this every day, every hour. You'll get so good at it that you will be able to wash gratitude over your body in a heartbeat.

The point of this practice is to retrain our consciousness to accept a "new normal". We are so attuned to fear we don't even realise that we accept fear and all its attendant emotions without question. We rush towards the first negative feeling and give ourselves over to it bodily. We need simply to attune to a higher vibrational state frequently enough that we make fear strange. We observe it, but we do not surrender to it.

When we feel fear, we don't even question its validity. Should this fear be here, or is it an impostor trying to keep me from my natural state of love? Gay Hendricks calls this the "upper limit problem".

The upper limit problem is this in a nutshell: our subconscious mind is programmed to accept a certain level of the good feelings. When it hits its upper limit, it will default to fear-based thoughts to bring us back into its comfort zone.[35] The subconscious mind is entirely impartial. It doesn't care what your program is; it will simply honour what is in that program. We must diligently do the work of raising the bar on our upper limit. We must retrain our subconscious mind to run a new program, one, which is attuned to the high vibrational states. Just as it feels strange at first to speak a new language, over time it becomes second nature. We can also attune to a higher capacity to receive the good stuff of life. In fact, the work of our lives is to burst through all upper limits and live in a continual state of bliss.

Forgiveness

The decision to let go our grievances against other people is the decision to see ourselves as we truly are, because any darkness we let blind us to another's perfection also blinds us to our own.

— Marianne Williamson

In many ways, I am saving the best for last by talking about forgiveness at the end of the book. "Forgiveness is a discernment between what is real and what is not real," says Marianne Williamson, the great contemporary teacher of the principles of *A Course in Miracles*.[36] Forgiveness is overcoming the belief in separation. Forgiveness is the meeting point of the three immutable laws, and the most spiritually fierce practice of all. This sacred practice brings all the laws into action. Knowing that all is one, that what is within us is reflected in the world, and that the vibration of the feeling state we carry determines the success of our lives, we can witness how invaluable it is to have a regular forgiveness practice. Practicing forgiveness with the same regularity as we practice gratitude takes us beyond ever feeling like we need to forgive. In other words, we stop believing that fear is even a possibility. This section on forgiveness also comes last as it will take all your spiritual fierceness to commit to forgiveness as a daily part of your life. Fear will fight for us and tell us that we need to be right, to maintain our grievances, not let others get away with things. As Marianne goes on to say, God doesn't need us to police the world. We must forgive if we desire to meet our true nature, which is love. Unforgiveness and love cannot co-exist, only one of them is real. We would have to be mad to say we believe in love and then maintain unforgiveness. We must forgive as an act of self-love. When we hold unforgiveness, we poison our consciousness with this low vibration.

Forgiveness is not the same as condoning. We do not forgive so we can be permissive of bad behaviour. We use our discernment to determine where it is best to spend our time and with whom. We do not have to leave with anger and unforgiveness. We can make a choice for love – for self-love and remove ourselves from situations, people, and places that are not in accordance with the high vibrations we want to inhabit. But we cannot argue with what has happened. Radical acceptance is the beginning of the forgiveness process. We must, as Byron Katie tells us, become a lover of *what is*, to stop resisting and begin changing disagreeable external circumstances.

What next? How do we move from these feelings of unforgiveness? With gratitude for what has been. Yes. Forgiving is really a willingness to see that the events of our lives have been in our service. From our human perspective, it might be impossible to see *how* this is so. Luckily, we don't need to see *how*, in order to accept, with faith, that this *is* so. Remember the cornerstone of intuitive intelligence is the belief that *I am a divine piece of God who is always working on my behalf*. At times, this requires all our spiritual fierceness to remember, but it is possible, especially with regular practice. The laws are impersonal – they exist whether we can conceptually engage with them or not.

Perhaps even more challenging than forgiving the other is forgiving ourselves. We judge, punish, reject, and shame ourselves more often than anyone else. We are unforgiving in the extreme when it comes to our own actions, and what makes this often so challenging is that this unforgiveness to the self-will masquerade as other heavy feeling states, so we don't even realise that this is what we are doing. Shame and guilt are the two most pronounced ways we will hide our feelings of unforgiveness towards ourselves. Pride, anger, and rage also work. No healing can happen until we have forgiven ourselves for our perceived failures and wrongdoings. The first step is to look at our fear. We hide our unforgiveness in layers of fear, and we need to look at it to recognise it. *I am angry because I am afraid I have done things that make me unforgivable,* for example. Forgiveness truly begins when we remember our true nature is love. The ego is trying to separate us from this truth by telling us that we have done things that cannot be forgiven by God. God cannot forgive, for God does not judge. This does not mean we do not behave in accordance with our true nature, which is love. It means that we are not held apart from God when we do behave out of accordance with love.

Forgive yourself for being vulnerable.

Forgive yourself for letting another hurt you.

Forgive yourself for the things you did when not of right mind.

Forgive yourself for not saying *no.*

Forgive yourself for not saying *yes.*

Forgive yourself for all the things you have accused yourself of.

Forgive yourself for all the things you have accused others of.

Forgive yourself now. Right now.

And if you don't know how, use the following practice.

The practice of forgiveness: ho'oponopono

Ho'oponopono is a Hawaiian practice of reconciliation and forgiveness created in its contemporary form by a Hawaiian psychologist and shamanic practitioner Dr. Ihaleakala Hew Len. We simply repeat four statements to ourselves, to the world, or to another to bring about the instant relief that forgiveness brings. This sacred practice brings all the laws into action. Knowing that all is one, that what is within us is reflected in the world, and that the vibration of the feeling state we carry determines the success of our lives, we can witness how invaluable it is to have a regular forgiveness practice. Practicing forgiveness with the same regularity as we practice gratitude takes us beyond ever feeling like we need to forgive. In other words, we stop judging. Ho'oponopono is simply magnificent, and I have found no greater forgiveness practice than this. Use it as a tool against any fearful thoughts and see how quickly you move back into a state of love.

Say and repeat *I'm sorry. Please forgive me. Thank you. I love you* in a loop. I use it like a mantra in meditation, or when I am walking, or during any mundane task, as well as when I can feel the fear of unforgiveness rising. What we are doing here is the ultimate act of humility, wherein we are acknowledging that everything we see in the other that causes us pain or grief is within us. We are defenceless before God. We are responsible for everything in our mind, even if it seems to be *out there.*

So if you are watching the News for example, and you see a story about something happening to vulnerable people in the world, and you are angry that it is happening, you can use this practice to take personal responsibility for the times and places where you have acted out of fear instead of love. This really is about taking responsibility for the first Hermetic law that I am one with all that there is. If I am able to be defenceless, to put down my need to be right and righteous (which shows up when we try to be God's policeman, to be the seeker of justice for all), and just surrender into that state of humility and vulnerability, then I have far more power to change the world.

I am sorry.

Please forgive me.

Thank you.

I love you.

Repentance. Forgiveness. Gratitude. Love. Say it over and over, mean it, and feel it. For there is nothing as powerful as love.

Chapter 6

Beyond a superficial spirituality to the path of the priestess

Where we are born into privilege, we are charged with dismantling any myth of supremacy.
— *Adrienne Maree Brown*[37]

What differentiates social activism from spiritual activism? Is spiritual activism just social activism done by spiritual people? No. Spiritual activism is informed by the shift in perception that happens when we have a deep spiritual practice; a shift that is inevitable if we are diving into devotion on a daily basis; a shift that raises consciousness. I have mentioned elsewhere in this book that as we pursue the path of intuitive intelligence, then we must be prepared for the reality that the things we desire will change. It is inevitable because we are shifting daily away from the ego-identified self into the Cathedral of the Heart. We will want to serve the greater good before all else. Our life becomes one of sacred service. Inevitably, our life becomes one of spiritual activism, too, for sacred service and spiritual activism are one. All genuine seekers of the soul will move from an individual spirituality to a collective spirituality. This is spiritual activism in action. Our inner work pours out of us into the world, and we yearn to make a shift for all, for we know, *I am that.*

In this chapter I am sharing my very personal experience of meeting a subconscious program that was so deeply buried within me that I was blind to it. Yet, it motivated all my actions and shaped my world. This subconscious program was that of white supremacy. I did not want to meet this program. I did not want to admit to it. I did not want to see what was hiding in my subconscious, and yet also in plain sight. But it turned out to be the greatest spiritual initiation of my life. It is the reason that the second edition of this book exists, and the reason I am now aware of my responsibility to speak about what deep spirituality and spiritual activism mean to me, and to take action in the world. Anywhere that I have unconscious biases, I am in fear. Supremacy is fear. Supremacy is the faulty belief that I am better than anyone else for any reason at all, but in this chapter I will focus on my experience of meeting my white supremacy, for this is such a dominant program that so many people on this planet at this time share. Whiteness is the 'norm' and anything other than white skin is treated as lesser than.

We are also diving deep into the archetype of the priestess in this chapter, because she is the archetype that exists at the intersection of a deeply rooted spirituality, and spiritual activism. The priestesses' spirituality is anchored in the world. It is a path that moves us beyond a superficial spirituality. Superficial spirituality leads us to believe that spiritual 'enlightenment' is attainment of individual success, and permits us to abdicate responsibility for the welfare of anyone or anything but our own self-centric reality. It is a perfor- mative spirituality that co-opts spiritual tropes to attain the appearance of wisdom, without doing the work of the spiritual seeker, and often through the cultural appropriation of indigenous people's faith and identity.

In this chapter we are also considering the antidotes to that superficial spirituality; two tools that are a powerful way engage with the world *as it is*, rather than to use our spiritual seeking as an excuse to bypass or disengage from the world. The world needs devoted spiritual action takers, and the action must be within us, and also in the world around us.

How did we get here?

It has been said again and again and again in different ways and in different places, that the world as we know it is coming to an end. The chaos is an end of life chaos as the systems of power that have worked for a few and kept most in bonds of slavery in one form or another, whether it be economic, religious, political or in fact literal slavery (which by the way is not simply a historical experience but one that is very present and real in our world today with an estimated 29 million people worldwide in bonds of slavery), collapse around us.

What has created this world is one terrifying idea that is now, I believe, and blessedly so, coming to an end, and bringing down the systems of power as it does. It is coming to an end because the collective consciousness is awakening rapidly. It is an idea that has caused all the harm that we experience individually and collectively. It is the ultimate weapon of the ego mind, and it has been exploited to create power for a few, whilst the majority are suppressed.

The idea is that of *separation*, in the West most potently expressed through the idea of individualism, which was first talked about in 19th century France, and is the proponent of the modern Western world - the world that is now crumbling around us. Individualism and the modern western world are ideas that have encouraged and rewarded self over service, the right of anyone to take at the expense of another or others, and that which has indoctrinated us with an adherence to competition over community. Charles Darwin's notion of 'survival of the fittest' contributed greatly to the creation of the current status of the world, and that of the last several centuries. Yet even for Darwin this was a theory only and not an absolute truth. Individualism in its most extreme form leads us to believe that we are without community, connection or shared experience leading, in part, to the mental health crisis we are experiencing in the West, the environmental destruction and many other iterations of a broken and sick collective consciousness. Self-determination, one of the aims of individualism, has turned instead into a total experience of disconnection, which allows us to behave in ways that are entirely selfish and harmful to others, as we falsely believe there is no consequence.

At the individual level this is a problem, but when an entire society is built upon this idea, when corporations, education systems and governments are built on this notion, the potential for harm and chaos is global. And that is exactly what we are experiencing.

The first tool – Rehumanising

We live in a time of chaos. Human consciousness is going through an enormous upleveling process, and those who can lead must. We must be prepared, as the great mystic Ken Wilber invites us, to shake the spiritual tree[38]. It is not enough for us to attain inner peace for ourselves. It is not enough for us to have our nice little lives and our comfort zones. We must take ourselves out into the world and offer what we have understood to those who are still in the darkness.

This may require us to dismantle our own lives, and it will always require us to change our relationship to the world, because the world is in desperate need of change. Spirituality is sometimes the gentle practices, and other times the fierce warrior energy that commands us into action in the world. Both these qualities are required if we're going to serve. Spiritual practices without a mandate of service mean nothing. This is also how we avoid the superficial, self-centric spirituality.

In my philosophy, as has been stated elsewhere in this book, human consciousness is like a computer simulation or dream state that supports us to awaken by giving us opportunities to move from fear to love. This shift from fear to love is what we are here for. I am speaking of *agape*, not human love by the way. Agape is defined as a universal, unconditional love that transcends and persists regardless of circumstance to become awakened Divine love. Love is all there is. That is the eternal truth, but we can hardly wrap our heads around that from a limited human perspective. This kind of love is what created the Cosmos, and it is fierce and it is unbreakable, and when it is invoked it will bring light to the darkest places. It is not one thing. It is Kali and it is Mother Mary. It is everything. Sometimes it is a comfort that nourishes and sometimes it destroys everything in its path, including us.

Once that inner revolution takes place we will be called to take action in the world. Once that fear program has been neutralised in our consciousness, we will yearn to see all our brothers and sisters receive their birthright, which is freedom, joy and equality. There is enough for everyone, but we have been programmed with stories of scarcity, lack and that life, including that of our Earth, does not have equal value. These falsehoods come crumbling down as we open into the Cathedral of our heart through our fierce devotion, and the separation myth is overcome.

Layla F. Saad, black feminist writer, racial justice advocate and spiritual thought-leader calls this the process of rehuman-isation. It is inevitable and necessary that we surrender into the heart to create a new paradigm.

If there is unmet fear within us that we are not willing to meet, then we are not spiritual activists, or even spiritual seekers. If there is any place within us that believes another person is lesser than us, then we are not in right mind or heart or soul with our spirituality. If we use our spirituality to divide and cause derision, then we have fear at work in us. We must go and meet our unmet fear, and then go deeper, and then go deeper than that. Anything that scares us in ourselves or in the world is an opportunity to get to know ourselves better. When we go and meet our fear we meet God or the Infinite in those places, and emancipate those places in others, and in ourselves. This is the process of rehumanisation, As I understand it, of the collective human heart.

My Rehumanisation

Audre Lorde a self-described "black, lesbian, mother, warrior, poet, said, "I am not free while any woman is unfree, even when her shackles are very different from my own."[39]

For those of us who have the privilege for any reason, which means we are free enough to pursue the soul, the responsibility of Lorde's words are real and undeniable. We have a power to change ourselves, to free ourselves from the shackles of the subconscious fear program of supremacy. This work cannot be avoided if we want to truly claim our place as spiritual seekers, leaders, and teachers.

I first heard Layla use the term *rehumanisation* when I was participating in her ground breaking #meandwhitesupremacy challenge. That challenge was part of the reason I knew I had to create a second edition of this book. It was a life changing experience for me to recognise that I had subconscious programs of white supremacy. I recognised the unhealed subconscious biases that I had never taken the time to meet, including the lack of intersectionality in my feminism, which meant I had erased and bypassed the experiences of black people, indigenous people and people of colour. Through the process of the challenge I recognised that I carry individual and collective racism, and that my public silence was causing harm to many people in the world, namely those who are not white. According to Layla the dehumanised heart is the reason we sustain a world in which so much racism, violence, disadvantage, and unnecessary suffering occurs; one in which personal success is privileged over a thriving community, or environment; in which no cost is too high to attain more individual wealth and to amass more power; and one in which people enslave other people and feel righteously justified to do so because of the colour of their skin.

Participating in Layla Saad's challenge was a watershed moment in my spiritual awakening (and the reason why I am focussing on race so specifically in this chapter, even though this chapter is an invitation to meet all supremacist beliefs as the fear programs that they are and to do the work to clear them). My heart was dehumanised at such deep levels that I had never consciously met myself, and as I showed up to do the work of the challenge, I was awoken[40].

All my life I have been on the path of spiritual seeking, to raise my consciousness, to experience agape. Yet, this stinking, festering wound was sitting right there in my heart, unnoticed. Unnoticed because the systems of power in the world privilege me as a white person, and so I literally did not see what was in plain sight. It was a shocking and overdue awakening, and it altered me like few things before it had. Engaging with the politics of race initiated me in to my sacred heart more readily than any spiritual program or text could have done. I did not anticipate that this would crack open my heart.

It's important to note that I am not encouraging us all to take up the mantle of spiritual activism so we get an accelerated awakening. We do this work because it is the work we must do. The very real side effect of rehumanising our hearts is the inevitable opening to the truth of agape, unconditional love. But our motive must be, *how may I serve?* How may I restore balance to the world so that those who have been abused and violated by the broken systems of power in this world can be restored to their rightful place?

Layla Saad activated my heart, but it didn't start that way for me. When I first encountered Layla's blogs[41] I was resistance itself. I was offended. I tried to count myself out of her accusations, and then I got angry. How dare she tell me that my spirituality was superficial, bypassing and violent? That wasn't me. She must be talking about other spiritual white women. I was defensive in the extreme, and I went through all the stages that I can see now were my ego attempting to maintain its power and privilege. Then at some point as I kept reading and researching, I could feel my resistance melting. I spent a lot of time talking things through with amazing women including Kym Seletto, whose patience and insightful reflection offered me a safe space to work through the things that I couldn't resolve in my head.

Through this process of speaking my fears out loud I could see that I was afraid of losing control, afraid of losing power. I was afraid of looking foolish. How could I have been so blind? I was brought to my knees in recognition of the truth. I had to let got of all my fears and do the work. I recognised that as the leader of an Institute that claims to train women as spiritual leaders that I had no public policy, no plan of action, and no education in my programs in regards to spiritual activism, anti-racism, inclusivity and intersectionality. More importantly I had not done the work of unpacking my white privilege. My silence was violent.

I was being invited to become congruent between my faith and my actions, and to stop excusing myself from the responsibility to take action in the world as a spiritual teacher and leader. I had to become defenceless and be unafraid to fall to my knees in deep apology. I could not stop there. I took action. I engaged the anti-racism consultation services of Sharyn Holmes[42], who created a detailed action plan for the Institute, and me, and I dived into Layla Saad's challenge, publicly sharing the darkest fears. The work must be done within, and in the world. There was absolutely nothing to be gained from guilt and shame, but I had to be prepared to now walk the path and take responsibility for changing the whitewashed world I inhabited. I became a patron of the work of Layla F Saad, Leesa Renee Hall and Sharyn Holmes through Patreon. I started following the work of spiritual black women and women of colour. I shared their work, I listened to their work, and I bought their work. I will continue to keep doing this work every day. I will keep unpacking my subconscious biases, until I can overcome the separation thinking upon which the world has been built for thousands of years.

I believe this is a moment available for all of us, and it is happening right now. It is the time to actively seek out our unconscious biases, in whatever form they take. Another layer of the collective subconscious of which we are all a part is offering itself up to be healed, to be witnessed, and to be returned to love. The dehumanised heart of all humanity is calling to be rehumanised, and so this is the time where all of us on the path of spiritual seeking must be willing to meet the world where it is at and contribute our awakening to the greater good.

We can accelerate the healing of this wounded belief because the energy is available. There is an invitation from the Infinite One Mind at this point in time for us to awaken to inherited, ancestral, genetic wounds that have sat unmet in our subconscious. We may have done this work on ourselves individually, but right now the collective unconscious is screaming out to be 'exorcised' to use Layla's term. It is time for unafraid to feel holy rage.

Holy Rage

Love is a bigger motivator than fear. We've all done more in the name of love than we have in the name of fear. We have taken more bold action in the name of love. We love the world so much that we are hurting when we see the injustices. Every emotional state we spend time in is programming the field, so if we are feeling great fear about the injustices of the world, and we never move beyond that, our fear and rage ends up contributing THAT to the collective consciousness. It is an act of inner discipline to hold a state of being that is greater than the evidence suggests. This is also the true nature of compassion. Compassion is a state of fearlessness. Gregg Braden defines compassion as, "...not an invitation to non-action or complacency...nor a license to sit idly, viewing the events of life from a perspective of non-involvement, numbness or denial. Becoming compassion is your invitation to immerse yourself fully into the experience of life, whatever the offering, from a place of non-judgment."[43]

We need to be able to transmute our fear into love in order to take right action. Until we do that we are using our fear as a justification for sitting in a low vibration and expecting things to be different. And the best way to do this is to start living in accordance with the hermetic laws. The laws, and the science of intuition, aka the true nature of what we are, means that we must take personal responsibility for the state of the world, and hold and enact a higher vision in order to see change happen. Sometimes that personal responsibility is to get enraged.

Those of us born into privilege by accident of our birth have the additional responsibility of training ourselves to dismantle the programs of supremacy that have been encoded into us through our genetic and ancestral lineage. We are born with the unique opportunity to stop taking our unnatural privilege for granted, and to do the sacred work, with great enthusiasm and humility for correcting the error.

We must understand we are not talking about human love. We are talking about divine love, I cannot reinforce this point enough, for it is a force far more powerful, the most powerful force in the Cosmos. It is in fact emotionally neutral, although we experience it as bliss in our bodies. Love is power.

We are by in large taught that it is not our job to stand up for the world. We are taught to be ordinary in the extreme.

Find a boyfriend or girlfriend, get married, make babies, get a mortgage, be a good employee, don't ask too many questions, get a car, upgrade that car. We are domesticated into believing that our own reality is all that matters. We are taught not to make trouble, except for agitating for the things that directly matter to our limited experience of life. We are taught from a very young age to live within very narrow expectations. So we dull ourselves to survive.

So when we see power, fierceness, fully expressed in another human being, some of us may never have met that before and we may find ourselves confronted because we ourselves have never loved with that kind of power. But that isn't a good enough reason to look away. It's a good opportunity to say, where am I unwilling to meet my own power? Where am I afraid of expressing holy rage?

In the same speech in which Audre Lorde stated that no woman is free until all women are free, she spoke at length about the power of anger to transform. She stated, "Any discussion among women about racism must include the recognition and the use of anger. This discussion must be direct and creative because it is crucial. We cannot allow our fear of anger to deflect us nor seduce us into settling for anything less than the hard work of excavating honesty; we must be quite serious about the choice of this topic and the angers entwined within it because, rest assured, our opponents are quite serious about their hatred of us and of what we are trying to do here."[44]

It is time to embody holy rage to burn away the delusion that has covered our gaze and subdued our truth, which is divine love. This love does not permit a world of great inequity. Holy rage returns us to our holiness. Our wholeness. We cannot awaken only to our individual self. We are one consciousness, masquerading as separate parts, and what we do to one part we do to all. This is the greatest delusion of all, to perceive separate parts of God when there is only one of us here.

The Symbol of the Priestess

The priestess is the symbol of holy power, an embodied power in service to the greater good. Her purpose is to support us to overcome the dream of separation through the development of spiritual sight.

Part of my life's work is to understand the responsibility of language. I don't use signs or symbols or words without great consideration of the multiple meanings and possible interpretations of these symbols. The use of the archetype of the Priestess is a carefully considered choice. The Priestess is the transpersonal bridge between the spiritual, energy realm and the earth bound, matter realm. It is vital work and it is THE work for this extraordinary time in which we live. The priestess is the deeply devoted spiritual woman in the world. Her work is different and unique to every woman. The Priestess is the symbol of those of us on this path of service being present in the world, rather than using our spirituality to shield or hide us away from the world. She is invested in creating change for the betterment of all and she is not afraid to get her hands dirty. Her mandate is service. Her service is not to indulge the trinkets and superstitions of the new age, but to consciously encode a reality for all that moves global consciousness from fear to love. The priestess is spiritually fierce.

By committing to spiritual fierceness, the path of the priestess, we are looking within to meet the Infinite. We must ask ourselves these questions; how deep is my devotion? How active is my faith? Do I have a deep, enduring and abiding practice that buoys me up to weather the storms of life, which will keep coming by the way, regardless of how devoted we are, because spirituality is not an insurance against the difficult events of life. But if our faith is practiced with devotion it will guard against constant disappointment. We will become deeply trusting of life. A good way to gauge the depth of our spirituality is to look at what we do in the privacy of our own life, when no one is looking. Devotion prepares us for whatever life presents including the shocking discovery that we have been complicit in a racist world, and that we carry the sins of the fathers in our subconscious minds, and that no matter how 'good' we think we are, we have a divine responsibility, by right of your birth, to get as uncomfortable as hell to serve the greater good.

The fear that exists in the world is an illusion, because 3D reality is an illusion. But it is a necessary illusion for it is how we train our consciousness. That is the very purpose of incarnating on Earth School and the very function of fear. I don't say fear is an illusion so we can bypass other people's experiences, but rather so that we will recognise that we have everything we need to meet it. The illusory nature of fear doesn't give us an opt out in having to participate in the very real problems of the world. What has created racism and all other social injustices is fear. And what will end the systemic injustices of the world is our willingness to go and meet that fear fearlessly, without thought for what we might lose, because we have already lost if we think we can attain enlightenment alone. We cannot. We are One Mind. And all must be returned to that state for any one to be returned to that state.

We must take the time to understand what we are arrived of. Sit with God and let that energy move our souls so that we may meet the places we have been holding ourselves back from love, because any block to love for another is us saying no to our own Infinite God nature. We must crave union with all life; let's turn our hearts back on. We must do the work to free consciousness collectively because we cannot be free in isolation.

The second tool - Spiritual Sight

Spiritual sight is intuitive intelligence. It is the ability to see both the material plane and the spiritual or formless, pure energy plane, concurrently. To be able to see the material plane through the plane of pure consciousness is, in my opinion, the greatest power we have, the greatest action we can take to move the world beyond the current state of affairs. This is not about cultivating a sight that takes us beyond the world, to bypass the current reality, but instead to bring us into a deep state of compassionate action – to see the failures and flaws in privileging the material plane. If we could see through formlessness to form – not the other way around – in order to see the coexistence of two worlds.

The overlaps, and more importantly the disconnections, of being able to hold two contrary states of sight at the same time allows us to take action at the level of form, which is informed by the spiritual or energy dimension first. We privilege our spiritual nature first as a result. What we want from this level powerfully contradicts what we want at the level of form. In other words to cultivate spiritual sight is to surrender the ego-identified self and to step into a bigger vision of who and what we are. It is to cultivate God Consciousness. Because much contemporary spirituality tells us that we are on the right track when we are focussed simply on the use of our spirituality to enhance the material plane, we have only seen through *form to formlessness*. What happens if we put our spiritual sight first?

There is no simple truth of reality. The dominant status quo of the world wants us to believe that things are simply the way that they are, and yet as we open to and privilege our spiritual sight we can see through this illusion to a greater reality, a higher truth, one in which we do not seek our advantage to the disadvantage of another. Spiritual sight, the coexistence of the mundane and the spiritual, at the very least keeps us uncomfortable enough to ask, why things are the way they are, and what else is possible.

The development of spiritual sight alongside of our ordinary sight is key to the development of a new paradigm of consciousness. If we use our spiritual sight to bypass, to overlook or top opt out of the current status of the world then we are causing more harm than good. We are causing as much harm as when we use the cultivation of spiritual sight simply to make the 3D reality better. Gary Renard calls this *moving furniture in a burning building*. Our spirituality is not meant to help us increase the nightmare of separation, to build more layers into the illusion. Our spiritual sight is our return to the One Mind and the coexistence of both human and divine sight gives us the ultimate power to make change for all humanity. This is why we wake up.

The Invitation

I am asking those of us who are ready to listen, to put down the trinkets and superstitions of a superficial spirituality, (which are probably culturally appropriated anyhow) and to stop distracting ourselves from the work. We must not be afraid of handing our lives over to this work. We won't miss out on what we think our spirituality is meant to bring us, although as I have said before, what we think we want will most likely change. We must give ourselves bodily to God because what God wants for our life is for us to meet ourselves as it. And that means returning to that state of holiness that can only come when we return to a state of wholeness. And wholeness cannot occur when we exclude anybody else from that vision. And that is what I had been doing, and now I vow to correct the error, to restore holiness to the world through understanding wholeness. Superficial spirituality, like white privilege or any other subconscious bias needs unpacking. Why have I believed man made dogma instead of going to meet myself as God? Perhaps the foundation of your spirituality was built on imitating what you saw around you and now you are invited to stop to question. This is the work of our lives. This is what spiritual seeking is. How may my spirituality contribute something greater to the world? I am here in service to something so much bigger than myself.

Fierce spirituality, what I call the path of the priestess, is built on radical acceptance of what is, not in the defence of the subconscious programs that keep us 'safe' (in other words benefitting from the current systemic power imbalances in the world). Radical acceptance allows us to stop arguing with what is and to start making change. The spiritual is and must be political. Just because these conversations are difficult to have in public spaces doesn't mean we don't need to have them. It is the difficulty that we have used as an excuse to not bring our spirituality into an active and public space.

If we are in hiding about being spiritual, in other words in our spiritual closet, then what chance do we have to bring light to the darkest and most unjust parts of the world as part of our spirituality? We instead speak about spirituality in covert ways, in terms of self-awareness, or wellness, or in increasing profitability in our business, in or in terms of how to work with ideas that are polite and mainstream enough to get away with. But this is not spiritual activism; this is not even true spirituality. Caroline Myss tells us that we have a responsibility to be spiritual revolutionaries, to be rebels, when we are born into freedom. She sites Jesus and Mohammed as spiritual revolutionaries. We are so afraid of losing our perceived power, status, acceptance, love, money or whatever it is, that we remain silent, even when it is killing us. Our silence is violent. We are not actioning our faith. We must out ourselves at the very least.

Please don't make this about goodness, and ignore the invitation. Look at the world globally. We are always given the conditions that support our awakening, collectively and individually. We need to look at our responsibility. Look at where we have been born. Look at our genetic and ancestral lineage. Look at what is sitting inside our subconscious by right of your birth. All of it gives us good information as to how we are being prepared to awaken. Be willing and unafraid. Be defenceless. If we want to be a force for good, if we want to be part of the revolution, if we want to be part of the awakening then that is where we need to go. Defencelessness will allow us to go with curiosity to the places we are otherwise afraid to investigate within. We don't want to be carrying this around any longer, because as the law of correspondence tells us *as within so without.*

Don't let naivety as spiritual bypassing allow us to pretend any longer this isn't happening. This is happening. The power systems are crumbling. And we can either be at the front as part of the change or we can sit back in our fear of judgement or doubt, or fear of the loss of power, and miss the opportunity to be part of one of the most important moments in human spiritual evolution.

There is no convenient time to do this work. If we've been hiding from our responsibility because of our obsession with our own busy-ness, and we claim to be on the spiritual path, then that time ends now. It may be terribly inconvenient and maybe things will have to change. Change is the only constant. But to lead that change to end any myths of supremacy, and to return us all to unified consciousness, overcoming the faulty belief in separation, well that is our divine privilege.

The practice: Take the Vow

To take a vow elevates our words beyond the ordinary and the mundane directly to the ears of God. The Spiritually Fierce vow is also a prayer than can be recited as often as needed, especially when we desire to gather our courage to us. When we pray we are inviting God into our life situation, and letting that grace move into us.

When we feel fear, we have two choices. Yet, only one is real. We can run and hide, which simply means we delay the time until we will have to meet this fear, so it not really a choice at all. Or we can gather our courage, and invite God to be with us through the recitation of these words. It doesn't matter what we are afraid of, whether it be previously buried subconscious biases, or the realisation that we have to leave a relationship, fear of losing something we love, or fear of failure.

Use this vow daily to bring about a change at the level of both the subconscious and conscious reasoning minds. As you repeat the words, bring your full attention to each word, and utter it with full devotion. It doesn't matter where you are, or when you do it, just make it part of your daily devotion. Once you begin to live in accordance with these words, you will be called to take action in the world. Don't ignore this call. Faith is active and must be demonstrated by our actions.

Let's take the vow:

I vow this day to meet my fear.

I vow to remember that I am unlimited, even when I feel separate and finite.

I commit to live with power and humility, strength and vulnerability, grace and grit, and to know that these qualities are the qualities of the Infinite, of which I am a divine piece.

I vow to live beyond the trinkets and superstitions of the new age.

I vow to remember that spiritually fierce is not just a phrase. Spiritually fierce is a movement of awakening consciousness of which I am vital part.

I give my life to the Infinite within me, above all else. I surrender all that is not of this truth.

I vow to live with the inner discipline, the soul fire that inspires me to choose Love first. Every, single time.

Conclusion

Before enlightenment, chopping wood and carrying water. After enlightenment, chopping wood and carrying water.

— Hsin Hsin Ming

Several years ago, I went on an amazing, life-changing, heart-opening, soul-cleansing yoga retreat in Ubud. I spent nine days in total bliss. I returned home with all of the best intentions to create a better life, a more peaceful home, a ridiculously happy marriage, and the most balanced children ever. Then the crisis struck - I mean, life happened. My old behaviour set in. The best way to deal with it all seemed to bury my head in the sand and ignore it. My partner was grumpy because he'd been on his own with two demanding kids, my kids were cranky because mum had been away for too long, work was piled high and I didn't understand how it was possible for a house to become so filthy in such a short amount of time. And all the while I was thinking, *why can't life be like yoga retreat? Why is all this going down just when*

I am so clearly moving into a deeper and fuller understanding of myself? Why is God trying to keep me from my peace?

Light bulb moment! And in fact, it was two light bulb moments:

1. This "crisis" was happening precisely because I was evolving. When we begin to move the emotional habits that have kept us limited, the ego will rush forward to invent new false realities to try and keep us down. It's simple. We will be most challenged when we are ready to let go of the big stuff. It doesn't have to work that way, but it often does, mostly because we human beings believe there has to be some kind of price paid for our happiness. When we let go of this belief, then the evolutionary steps in your soul's journey will be joyful. Because we understand now how our internal state manifests outwardly, we suddenly also meet a whole of bunch of events in the world that set off our fear.

2. There is nothing that is not spiritual. Here I was judging the yoga retreat as this place of great spiritual value, and everyday domestic life as the thing keeping me from my spirituality. This is not true. In fact, almost the opposite is true. It is easy to be "spiritual" when we are removed from the demands of the world and being waited upon hand and foot. This is not real life – not for me, anyway – but it is important to have time out from the demands of life. It is essential, in fact. The real work of the soul takes place in and amongst the distractions, demands, and joys of running a home, holding down a job, parenting, socialising, falling in and out of love etc. etc. etc. This is life.

This is life and there is a very good reason we have created it this way. There isn't one reason, of course. There are around seven billion reasons. Everyone's reality is as individual as they are, even when they are living the seeming exact same life as the person standing next to them. The reason for this is because our lives are handcrafted miracles, perfectly designed to facilitate maximum awakening of consciousness in this lifetime. We will all do this. It is unavoidable. What we determine, is how this awakening happens, how much joy or how much suffering.

There is no absolute truth. There is no one, right way to be spiritual. There is so much knowledge that comes under the banner of spirituality, so many ideas, many of them polemical. There is so much stuff to confuse, contradict, distract, complicate, and postpone our own intimate, unmediated relationship with God. My dearest hope is that this book is a guide on how to surrender beliefs that separate us from God, rather than adding more of a barrier between the Infinite and us. Belief is usually fearful. This book is a collection of tools on how to give up our fear, how to inhabit our spiritual fierceness. It is a series of ideas and practices that have served me to do just that. It draws on ancient wisdom and the teaching of modern mystics. It is a path to surrendering our limits so that we may return to what we are. Infinite, unlimited consciousness. Do you know, by now, that you are pure unlimited consciousness? This is the starting point for understanding our intuitive power. My very dearest intention is that you are closer to this truth than when we began, individually and collectively. The work of awakening to our unlimited selves is never for ourselves alone. Every time we meet our fear and make a choice for love, every time we overcome our belief in separation, we raise the consciousness of all. Seven billion people do not need to awaken. We just need to reach a tipping point. This is the spiritually fierce movement – to surrender our own unlimited selves on behalf of all humanity. The awakening of intuitive intelligence is the most powerful way to do this. When we live from our heart's intelligence we are operating from our unlimited all-is-one consciousness.

The reality is that there is *nothing* that is not spiritual, so no matter if we are washing the dishes or writing a spiritual text, we are doing the work of God. Don't avoid it. Just bring that perspective to it. We are always serving our spiritual awakening. Always, for that is the only thing we came here to do.

The very fastest way to do it?

We just need to be willing to hand ourselves over to God. *Thy will be done.*

Acknowledgements

This book has been created in partnership with the hundreds of students who have come through the doors of the Institute for Intuitive Intelligence, and so willingly allowed me to guide them towards their own unlimited consciousness. Their participation, experiences, and feedback have shaped the workshops and the content of this book. I am so grateful to all of you.

To my Third Level Priestesses who have taken the Institute to the next level, and shown me what I am capable of, by showing yourselves your own magnificence you are all spiritual leaders, and it has been my privilege to guide you on the path of awakening your intuitive intelligence and spiritual FIERCENESS.

Thank you for taking the Intuitive Intelligence Method out into the world so that the spiritual fierceness revolution grows. You are the ones who make this Institute real.

To my beloved for letting me go where you cannot go and letting me go there with grace. To my boys, who I know will know who they are because I have taken the time to know myself. To my mama and papa for giving me everything. To Angel, for being the first investor in the Institute and giving me the gift of living my purpose.

To my incredible business manager, inspiration, and friend, Laura Elkaslassy who sees what is possible and inspires me to go after it.

And to everyone who has played a part in the direct creation of this book, including Bec Mutch, Gabrielle Hall, Emma Turton, Victoria Crewes, Rachael Cannard, Michelle Whitehead, Raquel Dubois, and Mary Houston.

The second edition of this book has been inspired by the anti-racism and spiritual activism work of Sharyn Holmes. You can learn more about Sharyn's work here http://www.gutsygirl.com.au/. I am deeply grateful for Sharyn's commitment to this path of sacred activism and for being an example to me of how to do better.

About the Author

Ricci-Jane Adams Ph.D. is the principal of the Institute for Intuitive Intelligence®. She trains women all around the world as leading-edge intuitive guides, spiritual leaders and gold standard practitioners of the Intuitive Intelligence® Method. In decades of immersive learning and applied research, Ricci-Jane has created a system, which powerfully connects people to their unlimited consciousness.

Ricci-Jane is an award winning writer, speaker, and teacher. Her mission is to mainstream the intuitive sciences, and to teach people to know that they are God. Ricci-Jane has a doctorate from the University of Melbourne in magical realism. She is a qualified Transpersonal Counsellor, and has spent more than twenty years devoted to her spiritual awakening.

Endnotes

1. www.spiritualresearchfoundation.org
2. www.drjoedispenza.com/blog/consciousness/what-does-the-spike-in-the-schumann-resonance-mean/
3. See *Resilience From the Heart* by Gregg Braden.
4. See *Code of the Extraordinary Mind* by Vishen Lakhiani.
5. www.heartmath.org/research/science-of-the-heart/intuition-research
6. See *The Heart's Intelligence* by Institute for HeartMath.
7. *The Heart's Intelligence*
8. See www.watkinsmagazine.com/consciousness-in-the-cosmos-part-i-the-third-concept-of-consciousness
9. www.choprafoundation.org/science-consciousness/how-to-see-the-whole-universe-nonlocality-and-acausality
10. See Raymond Bradley et al. (2015) *Nonlocal Intuition in Entrepreneurs and Non-entrepreneurs: An Experimental Comparison Using Electrophysiological Measures*. Access here: noosphere.princeton.edu/papers/pdf/bradley.intuition.2007.pdf
11. See *Advanced Energy Anatomy* by Caroline Myss.
12. *Reveal: A Guide to Getting Spiritually Naked* by Meggan Watterson.
13. *The Art of Intuition* by Sophy Burnham.
14. See Raymond Bradley et al. (2015) *Nonlocal Intuition in Entrepreneurs and Non-entrepreneurs: An Experimental Comparison Using Electrophysiological Measures*. Access here: noosphere.princeton.edu/papers/pdf/bradley.intuition.2007.pdf
15. See *Key to Yourself* by Venice Bloodworth.
16. See *Key to Yourself*.
17. See *The Art of Intuition*.

18. See *A Return to Love* by Marianne Williamson.
19. The Institute is now called the Institute for Intuitive Intelligence.
20. See *Bridge Between Worlds* by Dan Millman and Doug Childers.
21. The Brotherhood of Light is described as a spiritual hierarchy guiding and serving the earth. The brotherhood is made up of angels and ascended masters. Divine beings have always guided human consciousness awakening and, at this time, the separation between the local and the nonlocal is even less distinct, and the support of the Brotherhood is readily available to those who open to it.
22. See www.headspace.com/science/meditation-benefits
23. See www.uncommonwisdomdaily.com/beat-stress-using-the-power-of-your-heart-20557
24. See Nick Ortner's website, *The Tapping Solution*
25. See *Outrageous Openness* by Tosha Silver.
26. See *Key to Yourself.*
27. See www.awakeninthedream.com/god-the-imagination/
28. See *Resilience from the Heart.*
29. See www.hermeticsource.info/the-kybalion-by-the-three-initiates.html
30. See Gabriel Cousens' http://treeoflifecenterus.com/
31. See http://www.independent.co.uk/news/world/world-history/the-eternal-female-worship-of-the-mother-goddess-1607599.html
32. See *A Course in Miracles*
33. See *Anatomy of the Spirit* by Caroline Myss.
34. See *Reveal* by Meggan Atterson
35. See *The Big Leap* by Gay Hendricks for more on the upper limit problem.
36. See *A Return to Love.*
37. http://sublevelmag.com/report-recommendations-for-us-right-now-from-a-future/
38. From *One Taste* by Ken Wilber. The full quote is as follows, 'And therefore, all of those for whom authentic transformation has deeply unseated their souls must, I believe, wrestle with the profound moral obligation to shout from the heart—perhaps quietly and gently, with tears of reluctance; perhaps with fierce fire and angry wisdom; perhaps with slow and careful analysis; perhaps by unshakable public example—but authentically always and absolutely carries a demand and duty: you must speak out, to the best of your ability, and shake the spiritual tree, and shine your headlights into the eyes of the complacent. You must let that radical realization rumble through your veins and rattle those around you'.
39. https://blackpast.org/1981-audre-lorde-uses-anger-women-responding-racism

40 The challenge #meandwhitesupremacy was a series of detailed and incredibly articulate instagram posts on the ways in which, and terms of use of, white supremacy is unleashed in the world, accompanied by deep and probing questions that we had to ask of ourselves and then share publicly on Layla's instagram account. This part was very important. Layla continually reminded us that doing this work privately or silently was counter to the purpose of the journey. White people remaining silent on racism, even when and especially when those same people considered themselves not to be racist is one of the most violent acts of racism). This is now available as a workbook at http://laylafsaad.com/meandwhitesupremacy-workbook/

41 http://laylafsaad.com/poetry-prose/white-women-white-supremacy-1

42 http://www.gutsygirl.com.au/

43 From *Walking between Worlds* by Gregg Braden

44 http://www.blackpast.org/1981-audre-lorde-uses-anger-women-responding-racism

The Intuitive Intelligence
Initiate Program

Loved the *Spiritually Fierce* book?

**Then join the program that guides you through the key
teachings of *Spiritually Fierce*.**

Do you know that you are pure, unlimited consciousness?

Are you willing to meet your subconscious fears and unlock
your innate divine power?

Meet your fear. Expand your true potential. Increase your
intuition.

There are ancient laws that govern the functioning of the entire
Universe, and a science to our sixth sense that can activate our
innate yet unrealised potential on every level. This knowledge
can be yours and with it comes the key to unlocking your
spiritual superpower... **Intuitive Intelligence®.**

Initiate is a celebrated, global online training program created by Ricci-Jane Adams. Hundreds of men and women all around the world have been initiated into their spiritual power, and now you can access it on demand.

The Intuitive Intelligence Initiate Program is a 12 week deep dive of weekly lectures and practices, combined with an online community that beautifully and powerfully scaffold you to succeed in truly living your intuitive intelligence.

This Training Program Can Exponentially Increase Your Intuition And Transform Your Life.

https://instituteforintuitiveintelligence.com/intuitive-intelligence-initiate-program/